Gro~ Naturally

A Teacher's Guide to Organic Gardening

Maggi Brown

SOUTHGATE

First published 1996 by
Southgate Publishers Ltd

Southgate Publishers Ltd
Glebe House, Church Street
Crediton, Devon EX17 2AF

Printed and bound in Great Britain by
Devonshire Press Ltd, Torquay, Devon.

British Library Cataloguing in Publication Data
A CIP catalogue record for this book is available
from the British Library.

ISBN 1–85741–022–X

CONTENTS

INTRODUCTION

What is Organic Gardening?

Young people today are very aware of environmental issues. Until recently they have not had much opportunity to put theory into practice. That invaluable resource, the school grounds, was maintained and controlled by the LEA. The pupils' use was confined to play and organised sport. New legislation, however, enables schools to be closely involved in the management of their surroundings. Barren expanses of asphalt, or gang-mown grass, are disappearing as schools take the opportunity to transform their surroundings.

Organic gardening activities offer teachers an exciting and environmentally valuable way of working in a wide range of curriculum areas whilst improving and developing the space around the school. The bleakness of concrete playgrounds can be transformed by even a small area of planting. The lives of children who play there may be enriched by creating and enjoying that planting, by observing it and the wildlife it attracts.

This book gives teachers the basic facts about organic gardening practices. It can be used by schools who are in the process of a whole site redevelopment, or it can be used by individual teachers, with little gardening knowledge, to work on the tatty flowerbeds under the reception class windows. Linked with ideas for investigations, activities and experiments, it enables pupils and teachers to fulfil many National Curriculum requirements whilst working together in a very creative and positive way.

Any garden may be managed organically: from the smallest collection of shrubs in pots to a complete allotment or purpose-built wildlife garden. The fundamental aim is to create a healthy, balanced environment in which the plants, the soil and the wildlife can be nurtured without using artificial chemical feeds, herbicides or pesticides.

This does not mean that such a garden is a tangle of weeds, with flowers and vegetables wrecked by voracious pests and decimating diseases. On the contrary, it can be even tidier and better organised than a non-organic one. Pests are controlled by the constant presence of natural

Recycling in practice.

predators and parasites ('the beneficials'). Diseases are controlled by careful cultivation, including rotational planting. Barriers deter other pests such as caterpillar-producing butterflies and grub-producing flies. Weeds, which deprive other plants of water and food, are removed before they can become established, or prevented from growing by mulching.

Plants which attract beneficial insects provide colour and interest throughout the year. Soil fertility and structure are maintained by the addition of home-produced compost, made from a variety of waste products. The micro-organisms present in healthy, well-composted soil allow plants to take up food when it is needed. This encourages sturdy, disease- and pest-resistant growth and optimum growing conditions.

Gardens controlled by, and reliant on, artificial chemicals are very different. The sprays which destroy the pests also tend to destroy the beneficial creatures, allowing an imbalance to occur. Pests have an awkward way of returning quickly in larger quantities. With few or no natural predators to control them, more and stronger chemicals are needed to keep them at bay.

An organic garden in a school's grounds provides a particular set of learning opportunities for staff as well as pupils. The overall school development plan may well come under review as a result of gardening activities. Organic gardening is inexpensive, environmentally beneficial to living creatures, and provides a classic example of sustainable development.

What are the benefits of an organic garden?

To the pupils:
- They will learn in ways that are practical and relevant. Maths, science, history, geography, art, design & technology will come alive.
- They will realise how important it is to be aware of our environment, even in the inner city areas.
- They will learn about the delicate balance of nature that man is in danger of damaging irrevocably.
- They will become involved in the physical side of school. The garden will be theirs, to be proud of and to care for.
- They will have fun!

To the staff:
- They will be able to cover a wide range of curriculum areas in an interesting and 'user-friendly' way.
- They might have fun too!
- Pupils whose literacy and numeracy need attention are likely to work enthusiastically in a garden, not realizing the skills they are using.

To the governors:
- Pupils will be learning creatively and positively. Where there is interest and commitment to the school, there is often a reduction in vandalism and behavioural problems.
- Gang mowing can be more expensive than the upkeep of a garden. A butterfly-attracting border around the school building costs less to maintain than neatly edged grass.
- Gardens are better than asphalt. Improvements to school grounds resulting in an attractive, educationally stimulating environment encourages parental support.

A chart showing some different control methods.

Pest/ Disease	Non-organic treatment	Organic treatment
Aphids	Chemical spray	Encourage beneficial insects; remove by hand; use insecticidal soap sprays on heavy infestations
Slugs	Poisonous pellets	Traps of beer/ protective barriers; encourage frogs and toads
Black Spot on roses	Anti-fungal spray	Remove and burn all infected leaves; grow resistant varieties
Red Spider Mite	Winter wash	Encourage beneficial insects

> **Did You Know**
> 50% of the national curriculum can be taught successfully in the school grounds. 15% needs an outdoor environment in order to be taught adequately.

CHAPTER ONE
Getting Started in Your School

Whatever the eventual size or shape of your organic garden, the initial stages and preparation are very important. A project such as this is often the brainchild of one teacher. In order to set up and successfully maintain an organic garden on a long term basis, the whole school needs to be interested, committed and organised.

The first step involves a public relations exercise, in which the idea is explained to staff, pupils, parents, governors, ancillary staff (the caretaker is a vital cog in this wheel!), the LEA as appropriate, grounds maintenance contractors and anyone else who will be involved or affected in any way.

It may well be that, without any formal organization, gardening activities start in a small way. If these increase in scale, there will undoubtedly come a time when it is likely that a more organized and coherent plan is required. Perhaps funds are needed for a large project, such as a pond, or a greenhouse. Whatever the reason, at some point a long-term development schedule should be planned. Where

The fruits of their labours.

ACTIVITY

Set up a display to show what you want, where you want it and why you want it. Use models, pictures, photos.

Look at problems to consider:
– Costs.
– Space constraints.
– Possible vandalism.

– As long as there is a suitable site, horticultural problems may usually be overcome.
– Can any parent with relevant qualifications help with the design?
– Does any parent have a demolition or skip business? (A wonderful source of left-over useful items.)
– Detailed and careful planning now should ensure long-term success.

such a schedule is in place, funds are more readily obtained. Local businesses, in particular, are often willing to help with gifts or small grants.

The equipment you'll need:

Equipment:	Use for:
pots	growing
boxes	growing; making compost bins
barrels	growing plants; mini pond
tubs	growing plants
plastic bottles	plant protectors
jars	soil studies
cardboard sheets (the larger the better)	mulching; lining compost bins
plastic sheeting	mulching; lining compost bins
old carpet (hessian-backed only)	mulching; protecting compost heap
timber	edging; compost bins
sticks	plant supports
netting	plant support and protection
wire netting	making compost bins; protecting plants
aluminium foil	reflecting light
a variety of growing media	growing plants
string	general use
bricks	pathways
tyres	plant containers

All schools can:
– Grow things inside on windowsills and benches.
– Have the windows open and see what comes in (friend or foe!).
– Explore the school grounds and see what plants grow where, and what creatures there are.

In addition, in a school with generous growing space, or with strip beds, you can:
– Create compost heaps.
– Make mini ponds.
– Clear ground organically.
– Have tubs of liquid plant food.
– Have a worm bin.
– Grow flowers.
– Grow vegetables.

In a school with strip beds, you may have to do this on a smaller scale. Design will be more complicated, and consultation probably more delicate.

In a school with only hard surface areas, with tubs, barrels, boxes (lined) and bins, you can still:
– Have a pond.
– Grow insect-attracting flowers and shrubs.
– Grow some vegetables (see list on page 52).
– Have worm bins (for plant food and recycling).
– Create liquid plant food.
– Make compost (in a tumbler type container).

Special problems for this type of school:
– Lack of soil in which to plant/grow.
– No obvious site for compost heap construction; liquid produced by the composting process needs to drain somewhere.
– Lack of secluded protected area to use for tubs, barrels, etc.
– Possible high levels of vandalism.
– Extra care and maintenance demanded by containers.

Possible solutions for this type of school:
There is often a secluded corner too inconvenient or small to be incorporated into the general play area. Can this be used for organic studies? Failing that, can an area of the main space be cordoned off? Containers made from recycled products such as old tyres and tied bundles of newspapers make perfectly suitable planting sites. The soft but tough material will also withstand playground activity without damaging the pupils! Compost may be made in a free-standing bin, supported on bricks to keep it off the ground, with a drainage tray underneath to catch excess moisture. Compost tumblers are ideal for this situation but they can be expensive.

Plants grow well in containers.

Containers made from old tyres and bundles of newspapers.

Above: Grow vegetables or flowers in tubs.

Below: Trees need large containers.

Plants to choose for containers

Select insect-attractant plants (see Plant List on pages 49-51) and fast-growing crops. A tub of nettles can be 'cropped' either to make liquid plant food, or to be added to a compost heap. The fresh young growth is high in nitrogen and very valuable. Crops to grow include radish, lettuce, courgettes, potatoes. All of these can be sown, grown and eaten within the spring and summer terms.

Shrubs and tubs

Shrubs and small trees do very well in tubs. They need regular feeding and watering, of course, but in an otherwise bare courtyard, they will provide colour and interest for the pupils as well as food and shelter for wildlife. The list of suitable varieties is enormous (see pages 49-51). Choose the plant for the situation and for the creatures you want to attract.

CHAPTER TWO

Ground Clearing

The usual reaction on being presented with an area of ground to clear is to reach for the bottle of weed-killer (herbicide). Herbicides are poisons. They may kill some weeds, but many of the most persistent, such as bindweed, couch-grass, and so on, have root systems able to withstand weedkillers. More, and stronger, herbicides have consequently been used, more frequently. Now these poisons have filtered through the soil and are appearing in our water system. Some weeds have developed resistance to herbicides. Some trees in urban areas have been killed by the cocktail of chemicals their roots have absorbed. The aim of the organic gardener is to work with nature, not fight it. Ground clearance the organic way requires patience and/or energy.

Mulch out the light

To survive, plants require light. If deprived of this, after a while they will die. The time taken depends on the species. Annual weeds such as chickweed can be killed in one growing season, as can grass. Perennial weeds, such as dandelion, couch grass, ground elder, bindweed, will be weakened after a season, but their root systems are good food storage units. They will require a much longer time without light. The area to be cleared should be covered with anything that excludes light, such as black polythene or large sheets of cardboard. Old carpet is another possibility, but avoid the foam-backed type as the foam disintegrates in the soil. Place the pile side next to the soil.

Planting through slits in the covering.

It is perfectly possible to plant through a light-excluding mulch to get some crops or flowers in the first season, but the ground needs to be warm. Wait until spring growth has really started, then cover the area to be cleared. Make slits for individual plants such as runner beans or courgettes or tomatoes and plant through the covering. Start some insect-attractant flowers off in pots and plant them out too. By September, the ground should be ready to use, so long as perennial weeds are removed. It is not worth putting down a mulch in the winter – unless plants are actively growing, they cannot be killed.

Hand-weeding

Dig over the area, removing weeds and their roots as you dig. Some roots are almost impossible to remove completely, they are so deep. Docks, thistles and dandelions are good examples. Broken roots will re-grow. Rotavation with a machine is very tempting as it is so quick, but every chopped piece of root makes another plant. Weed seeds can lie dormant in the soil for many years. During digging they are brought near the surface. They will germinate in the next growing season. A plot which has apparently been cleared by digging can therefore be disappointingly weedy after a short time. Many organic gardeners opt for a mixture of treatments. Thus the annual weeds are cleared by light exclusion during a growing season and surviving perennial weeds are dug persistently and regularly once the covering is lifted (and in the following seasons).

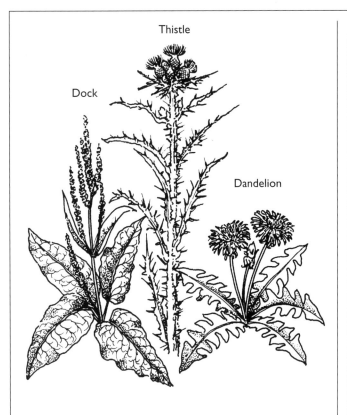

Thistle

Dock

Dandelion

Weed control

To control weeds in a garden the same ideas apply. Keep them covered with a light-excluding mulch of some sort and let them die. Bare soil may be covered temporarily with black plastic, and plants inserted through slits. Try a deep mulch of bark chippings, leaf-mould or newspaper covered with grass-mowings. Never let weeds go to seed. In one season, chickweed can produce 2000 seeds!

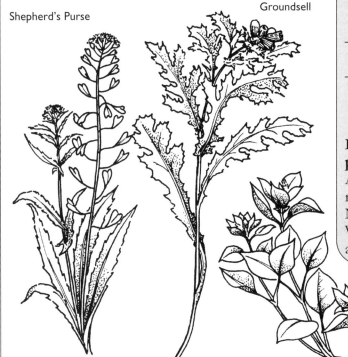

Shepherd's Purse

Groundsell

Chickweed

ACTIVITY

Cover patches of weeds or grass for varying lengths of time:
– How long before plant growth turns yellow?
– How long after re-exposure to light before growth becomes green again?
– How long before plants are severely damaged?
– Which plants fight back/take longest to die?
– Dig these up and compare root systems. (Thick, fleshy roots store food; thin roots do not.)

Pupils cover different areas with various materials and investigate:
– Materials used.
– Length of time taken to affect growth.
– Remaining growth.
– Soil temperature under mulches at different times of the year. Compare with bare, unmulched ground.
– What happens to weeds that are covered, but very near the edge of the covering?

How can you kill the weeds that have thick roots (see above)?
– Bury some roots in a pot of soil. Do they re-grow? If so, how long does it take?
– How many plants do you get? Chop the roots up and bury them again. How many plants grow from these chopped roots?
– Put the roots in a black plastic bag and tie up the top. Leave it outside for a day, a week, a month. See what happens. Compare the different results.
– Leave the roots out, exposed on concrete or another solid surface. Do they die? Re-grow?
– Compare the above treatments, using weeds with fine roots – e.g. Chickweed, Groundsell, Shepherd's Purse.

How does this method of weed control compare with hand-weeding?
An area is dug and all weeds are cleared by hand regularly during the time the other is covered. Nothing except hand-weeding is done.
Which area has fewer weeds after the same amount of time?

CHAPTER THREE

Preparing and Caring for the Soil

It is important to develop a programme of soil care wherever you start from and whatever garden you create. The addition of garden compost, rotted manure or leaf-mould to the soil will improve structure and fertility but in a new plot it is a good idea to test for specific nutrient deficiencies, soil type and pH.

Nutrient deficiencies

If your soil lacks particular plant nutrients, this can affect growth adversely and quite dramatically. Testing the soil will reveal any major shortages. Such tests may be done at a number of centres in the UK and any imbalance cured by the addition of an organically-based nutrient. (Refer to page 22)

The pH Scale.

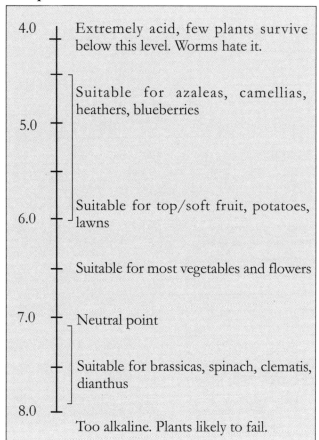

4.0	Extremely acid, few plants survive below this level. Worms hate it.
5.0	Suitable for azaleas, camellias, heathers, blueberries
6.0	Suitable for top/soft fruit, potatoes, lawns
	Suitable for most vegetables and flowers
7.0	Neutral point
	Suitable for brassicas, spinach, clematis, dianthus
8.0	Too alkaline. Plants likely to fail.

pH

The pH of soil is the measure of its acidity or alkalinity. It is important to know what your pH is. Some plants will not tolerate alkaline soils. Other plants will not tolerate acid soils. Some diseases are more likely to occur in a particular soil type. For example, brassicas grown in acid soil are more susceptible to club root. A soil that is too acid will have few earthworms as they hate such conditions.

Types of soil

Although there are many different soil types, their needs are fairly similar: plenty of organic material, which retains water, improves structure and provides food for plants. A sandy soil will warm up quickly in spring but will drain equally quickly, losing nutrients along with the water. Organic material is needed here to conserve moisture and plant food.

A clay soil will retain water and nutrients, but will stick together and take longer to warm up in the spring. It can be very hard to work when wet. The addition of organic matter will hold the tiny clay

Healthy soil makes the most of a confined bed.

particles apart, creating better drainage and a more open soil.

An old growing area which has been neglected will probably need as much preparation as a totally new site. In each case the addition of compost, well-rotted manure and leaf-mould will ensure soil improvement.

Cover your soil

Soil should be covered by plants as much as possible. This prevents precious nutrients from being washed out and protects the structure of the soil. In winter, clay soil can become waterlogged and puddled as air spaces between the particles fill up with water which cannot drain easily. Plant roots hold the soil open and allow excess water to drain away. Sandy soil can develop a crust as rain and wind pack the particles together. Plants break up this crust. Weeds can germinate in bare soil, too, whereas plenty of plants will crowd them out. In the growing season a mulch can be used around crops; for example, hay, leaf-mould or grass-mowings on a layer of newspaper. Always mulch onto warm moist soil as a mulch acts as insulation, preventing the conditions underneath from changing easily. Cold dry soil will remain like that for some time. Late spring, when the soil has warmed up, after some steady rain, is a good time to apply a mulch.

Mulch around a tree.

When nothing is growing, use a 'green manure' to protect the soil. This is a crop which is grown specifically for this purpose. It is then dug into the soil or hoed off when no longer required. There are many varieties. Choose the one which is most suitable for your particular situation.

> **Did you know**
> 1. It takes 200-1000 years to make 2.5 cm of top soil but only 16 years to lose it to wind and rain. Erosion is a major world-wide problem.
> 2. In one spoonful of soil there are more micro-organisms than there are people in the world.

Green manures.

'Green manure'	Nitrogen fixer? **	Sow	Dig in	Soil type
Winter Beans	✔	September–November	spring	heavy, wet conditions preferred
Buckwheat		March–August	after 3 months	can tolerate poor soils
Mustard *		March–September	can be used as a fast crop; after 3-8 weeks	moist, fertile soil needed
Phacelia		March–September	after 2 months, or over-winter	average
Grazing Rye		August–November	spring	moist

* Susceptible to club root. A member of the brassica family.

** Nitrogen fixer. As some plants grow, nodules of nitrogen develop on their roots. When the plant dies these nodules remain in the soil for the benefit of plants following on. Nitrogen is essential for plant growth.

There are other green manures available for different purposes and different times of the year.

Soil type

What soil have you got? Try the jam-jar test:
Half-fill a jar with soil, then top up with water. Put the lid on and shake very well. Allow the contents to settle. (This can take as long as 24 – 48 hours).
Examine the layers. There will be:
– A bottom layer of large particles.
– An intermediate layer of medium particles.
– A top layer of fine particles.
– A floating layer of organic material.

A sandy soil will look like this:

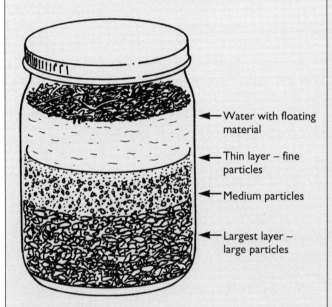

— Water with floating material

— Thin layer – fine particles

— Medium particles

— Largest layer – large particles

A clay soil often takes a long while to settle and separate, as the particles are so fine. It will look like this:

Water with floating material

Largest layer – fine particles

Thin layer – large particles

Bring soil in from other gardens, and other areas of the school grounds. Compare the soils.

If possible, dig a hole deep enough to see how soil changes according to depth:

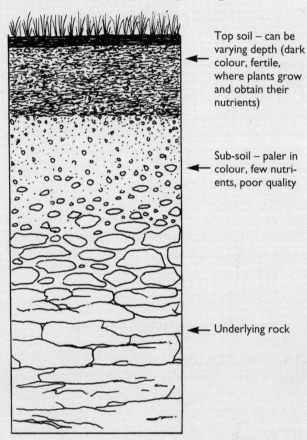

Top soil – can be varying depth (dark colour, fertile, where plants grow and obtain their nutrients)

Sub-soil – paler in colour, few nutrients, poor quality

Underlying rock

These three layers can be very shallow. The Cotswold area, for example, is limestone with a very thin covering of top soil. The underlying rock is easily seen when trees are uprooted or holes dug or fields ploughed.

Make shapes with the soil. Get a small quantity of soil. Moisten it. Try to make shapes out of it.
– Sandy soil will not hold long thin shapes, but will form a cone.
– Clay soil will make long 'worm' shapes.

pH

Test for pH. Testing kits may be purchased from garden centres. Take samples from different parts of the garden. Take samples from other gardens and compare.

CHAPTER FOUR

Recycling

Research has shown that up to 90% of the contents of an average dustbin can be recycled. About half of that 90% could be composted. The usual situation, of course, is that most household waste is removed and dumped in a land-fill site. These sites are ugly and can cause contamination over a wide area. Government legislation now expects local authorities to reduce their waste collection by 25% by the year 2000. Many local councils have instituted home composting schemes as part of that reduction, but it is surprising that many people still do not see composting as part of recycling.

The compost heap

There is nothing mystical about decomposition. The process is quite normal. What makes compost special is the combination of ingredients which, if separated, would not behave at all as they do when mixed. Put a pile of grass cuttings in a heap, and before long there is a slimy, black, unpleasant mess. A pile of twigs will remain a pile of twigs for a very long time. However, when mixed together, along with other material such as kitchen waste, animal manure and bedding, torn or shredded newspaper, (see Activity, page 16), these materials break down into a dark brown, friable, sweet-smelling substance looking rather like garden soil. This is compost. When added to a garden, it provides food for the plants and improves the structure of the soil in which they grow.

Artificial plant food encourages rapid, soft, lush growth which is an easy target for pests and prone to disease. Plants in well-composted ground draw their food as they require it and are usually much stronger and more sturdy in growth.

Conditions needed for making compost

Compost-making requires warmth, moisture (not sogginess – see Problems, page 17), air and a good balance of ingredients. Too much 'wet' material, such as grass and kitchen waste, and the heap will become compacted and soggy. Too many large, woody lumps and decomposition will take a long time. The mixing of ingredients enables the micro-

A wooden double compost heap – hot system.

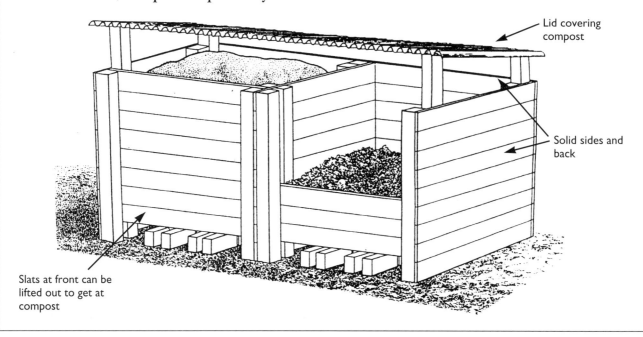

Lid covering compost

Solid sides and back

Slats at front can be lifted out to get at compost

organisms that are naturally present to move through all the material, devouring it as they go. This movement produces warmth, which speeds up the rate of decomposition. The compost is ready when the material is broken down, when it is crumbly and brown, smelling like soil, and when the components, apart from small pieces of twig, are quite unrecognisable.

Protection is needed

The heap should be protected from the elements in order to maintain conditions in which the micro-organisms thrive. Both drying out and over-wetting should be avoided. Apart from rain making the heap too wet and airless, valuable nutrients can be washed out of the compost. They are needed in the garden soil, not underneath the compost heap.

A compost heap can be a simple affair: a pile of material, mixed together on the ground, and covered over with old carpet or black polythene sheeting. Alternatively, a simple bin system can be installed. The illustrations below show some possibilities:

A Compost Heap

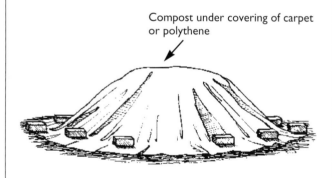

Compost under covering of carpet or polythene

Chicken wire lined with carpet or polythene. A covering of similar material on top.

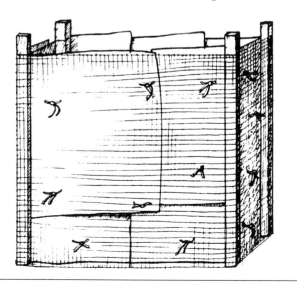

The basic ideas are the same in all cases:
– A good mix of ingredients.
– A covered heap, retaining moisture and any warmth.

The 'hot' heap

Compost can be ready in as little as eight weeks. If a large quantity of different materials is available and mixed together, the warmth created by the activity of the micro-organisms is such that decomposition is rapid.

A chart showing temperature variation with time

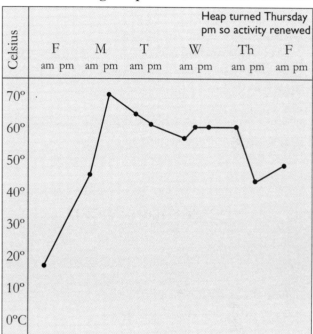

The temperature of the heap will rise sharply at first, then gradually decrease as material is processed. As it cools, different creatures take over the work. When the heap starts to cool, it should be re-mixed to get the material around the outer, cooler edges into the middle. The temperature will rise again as the process is repeated. After about 3–4 weeks, the heap will have lost most of its warmth and larger creatures will begin their work.

The 'cool' heap

Usually, however, a compost heap is created with a constant but slow supply of mixed materials. This style of heap may get slightly warm but will not reach the temperature described for the first method. Such a heap will take around 9–12 months to produce finished compost.

If possible a school should have two compost heaps. One which is being added to regularly, and one which is ready and is being used on the garden.

ACTIVITY
(very long term in this area)

Compostable materials:

What rots?	What does not rot?
vegetable waste	plastic
kitchen waste	metals
paper	glass
garden waste	stone
wood	other synthetic fabrics

N.B. – Avoid meat and meat-linked products (e.g. pies, gravy); they can attract vermin.
– Avoid diseased plant material.

Different contents for heaps
Note: Gloves should be worn at all times when handling any sort of rubbish or waste material.

Using two buckets full of each type of material, make three separate piles of:
– Wet material, e.g. lettuce leaves, cabbage leaves, carrot peelings, weeds.
– Dry material, e.g. hedge clippings, sawdust, woody plant stems.
– Mixed material, e.g. kitchen waste and weeds, old hay or straw, some shredded newspaper, some chopped twigs, some grass mowings.

Cover these different piles. After a week check for warmth, decomposition, etc.
– Which heap is warmer?
– Which is most decomposed?
– Which heap is least decomposed?
– Which heap is nicer (smell and texture)?

Continue checking these heaps for differences in decomposition and temperature. Monitor weekly. When all activity seems to have ceased, the different material can be added to the main heap for complete composting.

A quick heap
Construct a compost bin a square metre in size. If at all possible, gather enough material (see above list) all at once to fill the bin. It might be necessary to enlist more than a single class to achieve this.
– Mix all the material together.
– Fill the bin.
– Measure the height of the material above the bottom of the bin. Put the cover on and leave alone.

Section through a filled compost bin

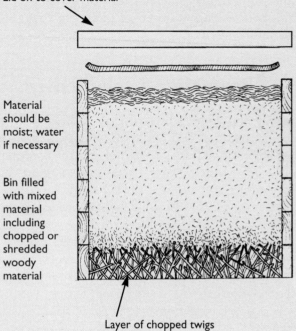

Lid on to cover material

Material should be moist; water if necessary

Bin filled with mixed material including chopped or shredded woody material

Layer of chopped twigs

– Check the temperature regularly – use a soil thermometer if possible.
– What is the highest temperature reached?
– After how many days?
– What happens to the height of the material when the heap starts to cool? (It should decrease in size as the material breaks down.)
– Turn the heap so that the material at the side goes to the middle. If you have several bins, this is easy to do. Just transfer the outer material to another bin, and pile the previous inner material over the top. Again, measure the height of the material above the bottom of the bin.
– Monitor the temperature again.
– As the heap cools, check the height of the material. What did you start with? What have you got now?
– After the heap has been turned and it has again cooled, look at the material. Can you see what it started as? What is most/least decomposed?
– Are there creatures present? (worms, beetles, centipedes?)
– If the bin has been filled in one go, how long did it take for material to be well broken down?

If pupils find it difficult to understand how the creatures got in, the teacher might have a dialogue something like this:
"Teacher: What have we put in the bin?
Pupil: Garden rubbish.

Teacher: Where do creatures live?
Pupil: In the garden.
Teacher: How did they get in the bin then?
Pupil: We put them in when we put the rubbish in.
Teacher: What is the rubbish on?
Pupil: The ground.
Teacher: What creatures live in the ground?
Pupil: Worms, etc.
Teacher: How do the worms get into the rubbish?
Pupil: Through the ground."

Note: If the weather is cold and wet, you can insulate the heap with recycled 'bubble-wrap' packing material. Even in winter a well-mixed heap will heat up quickly if insulated.

A slow heap
– Construct a bin. Decide – will this compost be only from the school, or will pupils contribute?
– Before putting anything else in, put a layer (about 5cm deep) of twigs/woody stems over the base area. This gives the slow heap a layer of air.
– Add whatever suitable material is available to the bin as it occurs. Make sure you mix 'wet' materials with absorbent ones, e.g. weeds/cabbage/lettuce leaves need hay/straw/newspaper in with them. Chopped up prunings need to be mixed with wetter material.
– Avoid thick layers of any one material. Always mix large quantities of waste into the existing heap with a fork.
– Keep a record of what goes into the heap.
– Check the temperature regularly – especially before adding new material, then 24–36 hours later. Is there a difference?

After about 12 months, this 'cold' heap should be ready to use. Pull the material out with a rake or fork. Return to be re-composted all lumps not adequately broken down. The rest should be either used in the garden, or stored in medium-sized sacks (30 litres) in a cool, dry place until required. Can you distinguish what went into the heap? If so, it may not yet be ready.

Problems

The wet, smelly heap
A compost heap consisting largely of kitchen waste and green garden waste will often become wet and smelly. The material is so high in water and low in absorbent material that it rots down quickly and becomes airless and dense. This problem may be overcome by adding dryish, absorbent material such as paper, old hay and straw, or shredded woody prunings. Drag the wet material out and mix everything thoroughly, then pile it all back.

The dry heap
A heap which is cold and not decomposing or reducing in size may be too dry. If you think this is the case, add some green material such as grass mowings or fresh weeds, and water it fairly well to make everything moist, not saturated. Woody prunings should be chopped or shredded so that they can decompose faster.

Leaf-mould

When stacked in quantity, and allowed to decompose, deciduous autumn leaves turn into a superb soil conditioner. This usually takes between one and two years. Therefore, it is sensible to have two or even three leaf-mould bins. These are different from compost bins. Leaves don't need warmth to decompose, and it does not matter if they get wet. They break down differently, in a slow, cool way.

A leaf-mould bin

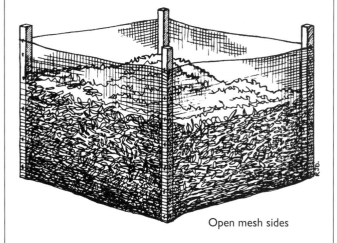

No cover required

Open mesh sides

They should be moist when put in the bin – if necessary water them, or collect after rain. Big leaves tend to stick to each other and take a long time to break down. The whole process can be speeded up by adding nitrogen in the form of fresh grass mowings. If this is mixed into the leaf pile, leaf-mould may be produced in about 12 months, as the bacteria in the mowings accelerate the decomposition.

- Collect deciduous autumn leaves.
- Stack them in a bin or bins. They could go in black plastic sacks if there is no other space that is available.
- Measure the height and temperature of the leaf stack.
- Monitor these measurements. Do they change rapidly? Slowly? At all? At a constant rate?
- Do different sorts of leaves break down at different rates?

If you have two bins in one year, add nitrogen (grass clippings) to one bin and not the other.
- Monitor the two bins for the differences that result from adding the nitrogen, particularly the rate of change.

When the leaves have turned into a dark brown, coarse material, they are ready for use. Now you will be able to use them to improve the quality and structure of the soil by digging in or spreading as a mulch. Mixed with organic fertilisers, leaf-mould can be used as a growing medium for seeds and plants.

Any deciduous leaves may be turned into leaf-mould. Large leaves such as horse chestnut or sycamore can sometimes pack together and take a long time to break down. Run the lawn mower over them to chop them up a bit before putting them in the bin. This will help them rot faster.

Avoid evergreen leaves, such as conifer clippings, holly and laurel. Compost them separately until they become brown, then add them to the compost heap. They do not break down properly in a leaf-mould bin.

To see what difference, if any, there is to plant growth when leaf-mould is added to the soil:
- Set up a trial of three plots, beds or tubs.
- Grow vegetables such as onions or potatoes. The difference is easier to see.

Plot 1. Improve soil with organic fertiliser only.
Plot 2. Improve soil with organic fertiliser and green manures.
Plot 3. Improve soil with leaf-mould and organic fertiliser.
How do the plots or tubs compare? Measure leaf growth and final yield.

Leaf-mould in preparation.

CHAPTER FIVE

Worm Composting

This is an ideal activity for schools with no space for a garden in which to site an ordinary compost heap. However, some people dislike worms, and it might be problematic to obtain whole class participation. Some thought will also need to be given to caring for them during the Easter and summer holidays. In the winter they require little if any food.

Worm compost makes an excellent plant food. Use it inside, on house plants, or outside as a general fertiliser. It replaces artificial, chemically produced plant foods and is especially useful for plants in containers.

The worms concerned are not ordinary garden worms but brandling worms (*Eisenia foetida*). They occur naturally in manure heaps and mature compost heaps but can be cared for in a suitable container, where they will process food scraps and other waste. There are many worm bins on the market now but it is quite easy to make your own. Worms may be purchased commercially, or, if you know a local farmer, he may let you have some from a manure heap.

Brandling, or Tiger worms (*Eisenia foetida*).

Insulated wooden bin, able to remain outside all year. Insulation for an outside bin should be 2.5cms. There is no perfect size. If the bin is to be outside permanently, then a 90cms cube is good. If the bin is indoors, then the container can be almost any size.

Below: Shallow wooden worm bin. Free standing.

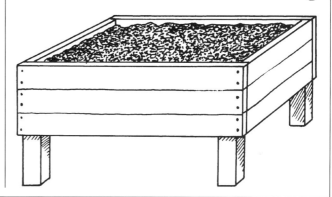

Worm bin adapted from a dustbin.

Both the shallow wooden worm bin and the compressed paper bin will need shelter in winter.

Essential requirements for worms

Worms need air
They work near the surface so a bin with a large surface area is best. If you convert a large plastic dustbin make plenty of air holes in the lid and around the top edge, but make sure that rain cannot get in and soak the worms.

Worms need moisture
If the worm dries out it will die. The skin must be moist for it to breathe. Keep the surface of the compost covered with a thick layer of moist newspaper. Take care to avoid water-logging; that is just as problematic. Worms can drown.

Worms need the right temperature
If they freeze or bake they will die. The ideal temperature is between 18° and 25° Celsius, but they remain active between 10° and 29°C. An insulated worm bin can remain outside permanently. During extreme weather conditions, the worms will bury themselves in the safety of the deepest compost.

Worms need darkness
If exposed to light, the worms will retreat to the nearest dark place. You can make use of this when you need to separate the worms from the compost.

Spread some compost out, fairly thinly, on a surface. Cover up half with wet newspaper. Leave it for some hours. All the worms present will move from the uncovered compost to the covered compost.

Worms need food
Most kitchen waste can be fed to the worms, as well as a little garden rubbish, such as annual weeds. They prefer softish food. Large lumps of tough, raw root vegetables will take a long time to be broken down. Avoid meat products as they tend to rot and can attract flies. Avoid onions and citrus peel. This material can create acid conditions which worms dislike.

Feeding the worms

Food should be placed on the surface of the worm compost, in a layer not more than 5cm deep. Little and often is the ideal feeding pattern. Do not cover the whole surface. Leave a quarter free so that the worms can escape if they find conditions uncongenial for any reason. Add more food when the worms are working all over that which is already there. Alternatively, bury food in small batches. Rotate the location of these batches around the bin each time you add food.

Setting up a worm bin

If you use a deep plastic bin:
– Put a layer about 10cm deep of sand and gravel in the bottom of the bin. This acts as a drainage layer.
– Place a perforated board on top of the gravel. Any excess liquid from the worm compost will drain through the holes and not drown the worms.
– On top of the board, place a 10cm layer of shredded paper. Newspaper is fine, but avoid coloured inks as they could be toxic.
– On top of the paper, place the worms in their bedding. Bedding can be leaf-mould, compost or rotted farmyard manure. Whatever the worms are in, just put everything on top of the paper.
– Cover the surface of the bedding with a thick layer of thoroughly moistened newspaper. Put the lid on the bin.
– Let the worms settle for a few days, then start to add food, in small quantities for the first week.

If you use a shallow container:
Some containers, such as shallow boxes or reconstituted paper bins do not need a drainage layer.

Excess moisture is able to evaporate through the wood or paper.

– Put a layer of well-moistened paper on the bottom of the container.
– Pile the worms and their bedding on top of this.
– Cover with more well-moistened newspaper and put the lid on the bin.
– Feed as already described.

Care in winter

If worms are inside in winter, and warm, they will continue to work and therefore need feeding as normal. If they are outside or in a cool place such as a shed or greenhouse, they will need little if any food. Cool conditions slow down their activity. Food will be consumed slowly if at all. Large amounts left on the surface can putrefy and may cause problems. Suspend feeding when food is obviously not being processed. Remove any surplus food. Put in a layer of partly decomposed compost or some well-rotted manure. Leave the bin like this until the weather starts to warm up. Check from time to time and, if the worms seem very active, add some more compost or manure. Start feeding again in the spring.

Care during holidays

Worms kept inside will need to be fed throughout all holiday periods. Fortunately, worm bins are fairly easy to transport.

Worms kept outside in insulated bins will not need feeding over Christmas. They will possibly need food during the spring half-term holiday, especially if the weather is mild, and certainly during all other holiday times. They must not be allowed to dry out. This is particularly important during the summer. A layer of damp newspaper will protect them for a day or two, but arrangements must be made for regular attention before a worm bin is set up.

What goes wrong

If, when the bin is opened, the worms are all up the sides and on the lid:
– Check that the compost is not water-logged. They can drown. If it appears to be very soggy, add some shredded paper to absorb moisture. Push it into the worm compost to soak up excess liquid.
– Check that there are not too many worms. Start another bin if you have a seething mass. In warm weather worms can breed rapidly.
– Make sure they are getting enough to eat. A large colony of worms will devour an inch layer of food in a day.
– Make sure the conditions are not too acid. Add dried, crushed eggshells, ground limestone (dolomite), or calcified seaweed which will help overcome this.

If when the bin is opened, all the worms are dead:
– Check for water-logging.
– Check the food given. Pesticides on vegetables can be a problem as worms are very sensitive.

There is still a lot to learn about keeping worms in bins. It may be necessary to contact the experts for advice, although even they do not always have an instant answer. Write (not phone) to the HDRA (see address at back).

Did you know
Worms have no teeth. Food is sucked in, then ground by stones in the gizzard before being digested, and the waste (worm compost) is excreted.

ACTIVITY

Set up a worm bin:
– If possible, examine a working worm bin. Try to find several different types. Your local allotment society may be able to help.
– Decide on the style of bin.
– Decide on the site for the bin.

What will worms process fastest?
– Uncooked potatoes, carrots, swede.
– Lettuce leaves, cabbage leaves, carrot peelings.
– Mashed potato, bread, cooked rice, soggy cereal.

Decide how to measure the quantity in order to obtain a scale to measure the results.

Use finished worm compost as plant food:
– Test the efficiency of the compost as food by using three (or more) identical plants, in different pots, with different amounts of worm compost. Measure the growth rate, number of flowers and fruits.
– Try one plant in pure worm compost. (It may well die – the compost is usually too rich.)

Original Organics produce purpose-built worm composters, see page 56.

Liquid Plant Food

(This section is particularly suitable for schools with no garden space.)

Many pupils (and teachers) will be aware of the wide range of liquid plant foods available commercially. While plants in a well-composted soil should not need extra feeding, there are some exceptions. Hanging baskets, where the proportion of plants to growing medium is out of balance, need regular attention, as do some greedy, fast-growing plants such as tomatoes and cucumbers. It is perfectly possible to create a liquid feed, without using artificial chemicals.

Which plants make food

Both nettles and comfrey leaves may be turned into plant food. Nettles are rich in a wide variety of minerals. Comfrey (*Symphytum x uplandicum*) is rich in potash, which is needed to produce good fruit. The leaves of both these plants break down quickly when placed in containers with or without water. Nettles are easily available. Comfrey plants may be grown in an out-of-the-way corner. They are very deep-rooted perennial plants. The best variety for gardening purposes is 'Bocking 14'. This can be obtained from the mail order catalogue of the HDRA.

Comfrey

Nettles

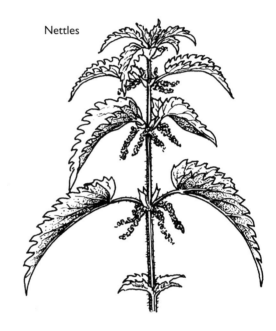

ACTIVITY

To make ready-to-use liquid:
Ideally, use large containers such as a rain barrel with a tap at the bottom. If this is not a practical possibility, then small bins with clip-on lids will do instead.

– Nettles produce a very smelly, highly nutritious feed, rich in many minerals and ideal for feeding any plants.
– Comfrey produces a feed high in potash – an excellent food for hanging baskets, tomatoes, cucumbers and similar greedy plants.

Method
1. Nettles – Put 1kg fresh nettles in 10 litres water. Leave for about two weeks. Use diluted 1:10.
2. Comfrey – Put the leaves and water in the barrel. Add 7kg leaves to 100 litres of water. Allow to infuse. After 4 – 6 weeks there will be a foul smelling, light brown liquid. Does not need diluting.

Comfrey/Nettle concentrate

It is possible to make a concentrate using either of these plants. Just use the leaves from the plants with no added water. Pack them into a container and allow them to break down. The resulting liquid does not smell so much and, diluted, makes a superb plant food. Comfrey liquid, high in potash, is particularly good for tomatoes and other greenhouse crops which ripen quickly and are greedy for nutrients. Dilute 1 part concentrate to 15 parts water before use.

ACTIVITY

- Try out different feeds with the same types of plants. Water some tomatoes with comfrey liquid, some with nettle liquid, some with plain water.
- Do the same for pots/baskets of flowers and indoor plants.
- Measure growth rate, bushiness, abundance of flower and fruit.

Container packed with Comfrey/Nettle leaves.

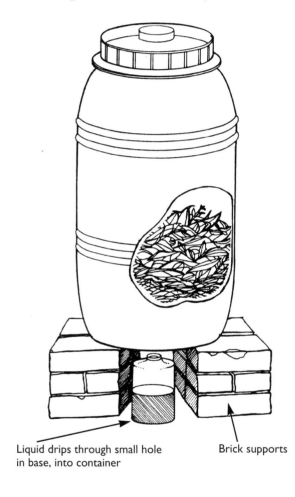

Liquid drips through small hole in base, into container

Brick supports

Container packed with leaves and water.

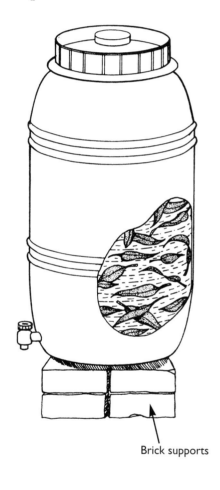

Brick supports

Comfrey (*Symphytum x uplandicum*) is easy to grow. It does best on deep, rich soil in full sun but it will grow even in a partially shaded site. It does need deep soil. The roots can go down 2-3m. Comfrey dies down in the winter and re-grows in the spring. It is an excellent source of potassium which is one of the main plant nutrients. Once established, you can cut the leaves several times a year. These can be used to make liquid fertilizer, or added to the compost heap, or used as a mulch around other plants. Comfrey has been used for hundreds of years as a herbal treatment. Its common name 'Knitbone'

indicates usefulness in the treatment of injuries. Even now comfrey ointment is used to reduce the pain of bruises and sprains.

Investigation

How many everyday herbs used in modern kitchens have a history of medicinal use? What would the Romans or Tudors or Victorians have used to treat illnesses and injuries?

CHAPTER SEVEN

Pest Control

arden pests and diseases are not a modern problem. The Victorian farmer and gardener suffered from slugs and greenfly just as we do. Remedies listed in some of the gardening books of the time are fascinating. Some of the potions quoted are also highly toxic to humans (and illegal now). Organic gardeners accept the need to use certain products occasionally to control garden problems. These products, however, are of natural origin and break down very quickly in the environment. They leave no long-lasting residues on fruit or vegetables, and are only used when a problem has become too difficult to control in any other way. It is not always necessary, however, to spray a problem away, there are many other remedies.

Encourage natural predators

Most of the creatures we consider a problem in the garden could be kept in check by their natural predators. Nature usually maintains a fine balance between pests and their predators. Problems arise due to mankind's manipulation of, and interference with, this balance.

Traps and enticers

These are generally used for pests such as slugs, earwigs, wire worms, moths and so on. The idea is to entice the creature into an accessible place, after which it can be moved elsewhere, or 'dealt with'.

What eats what in the organic garden?

Beneficials → Pests ↓	Frogs	Lady-birds	Lace-wings	Hover-fly larvae	Wasps	Anth-ocorid bugs	Black beetles	Para-sitic wasps	Hedge-hogs	Birds	Spiders
Aphids	●	●	●	●			●	●		●	
Caterpillars		●	●		●	●	●			●	●
Slugs	●						●		●	●	
Snails	●									●	
Mites		●		●	●	●				●	●
White fly								●		●	
Woodlice	●								●	●	
Vine Weevil larvae							●				
Capsid bugs						●				●	
Millipedes	●								●	●	

Holes for slugs to enter

Holes 2cm above soil level to prevent ground beetles from drowning

Soil

Container with lid containing slug attractant liquid.

Earwig trap

An upside down flower pot stuffed with straw on a bamboo cane makes a good earwig trap

– Wood lice can be enticed into scooped out oranges or cooked potatoes.
– Yellow sticky traps, available from most garden stores, will catch many flying insects.
– Wire-worm can be enticed into pieces of raw potato or carrot spiked on sticks sunk in the soil.
– Moths can be enticed into pheromone (hormone scented) traps. Buy these traps in good garden centres, or from the HDRA catalogue. Scent refills can also be purchased.

Pheromone trap.

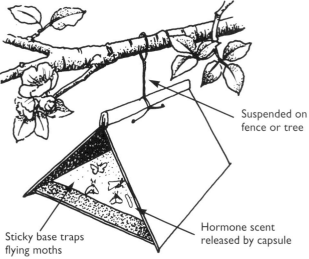

Suspended on fence or tree

Sticky base traps flying moths

Hormone scent released by capsule

Barriers

These can be used against a wide range of pests, both flying and crawling. Sticky bands around the trunks of fruit trees will prevent moth caterpillars and wingless females from crossing. These pests damage leaves, buds, young shoots and fruit. The sticky band is usually made of grease, and is sold already prepared.

A grease band

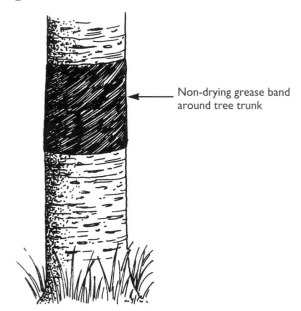

Non-drying grease band around tree trunk

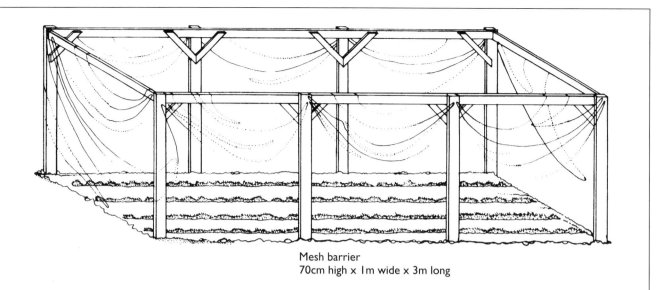

Mesh barrier
70cm high x 1m wide x 3m long

Mesh barrier

A fine mesh barrier around carrots will prevent carrot root fly from laying eggs. The female usually flies just above ground level. On reaching carrots she lays her eggs which hatch into larvae, the small maggots that we find tunnelled in carrots occasionally. If the female hits the barrier mesh, she is forced up and over. By the time she drops down near to the ground again, the carrots are far behind.

Carpet underlay

A small square of carpet underlay around the stem of brassica plants at ground level prevents cabbage root fly from laying eggs. This technique can be used to protect cabbages, kale, sprouts, and so on.

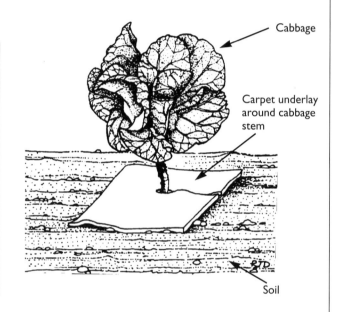

Cabbage

Carpet underlay around cabbage stem

Soil

Metal cloche hoops and covering.

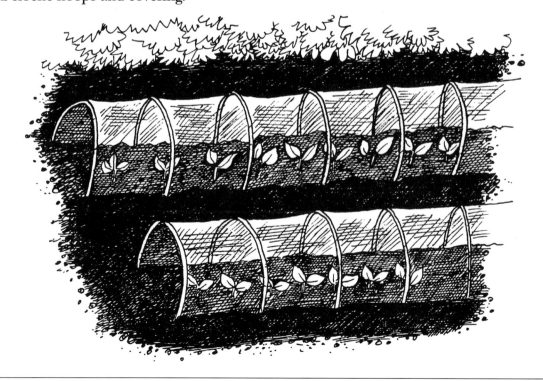

Fleece covering crops.

Birds, moths and butterflies can be kept off by covering crops with netting of various sizes, supported on a wooden frame, or on metal cloche hoops.

Fine mesh or horticultural fleece can prevent aphids from either damaging crops directly or transmitting diseases (e.g. Cucumber Mosaic Virus). As the mesh or fleece can prevent pollination, care and thought are necessary if a crop is to be covered for any length of time. Try hand pollination where necessary.

Time your planting

Some crops may be protected from attack by planting at a particular time in order to avoid certain pests. Peas should be sown early or late, so that they are not in flower in June, when the Pea Moth is looking for flowers in which to lay its eggs. Think about harvesting times and holiday dates, too.

Organic sprays and their applications.

Spray	Controls....
Derris	aphids, caterpillars and other pests
Insectidal Soap	aphids, white fly, spider mites
Pyrethrum	aphids, small caterpillars, sawflies
Soft Soap	aphids
Read the label before you buy. Use pesticides safely.	

Biological control of pests

Recently, more and more use is being made of biological control of certain pests in preference to the use of pesticides. Aphids, white fly, red spider mite and many other problem creatures all have their own naturally occurring predators. Modern technology has made it possible to breed these in large quantitites, store them and transport them safely to wherever they are needed. Biological control tips the balance towards the grower by out-numbering some of the pests.

Advantages of biological control:
– No build-up by pests of resistance to chemical treatments.
– No poisonous residues on food or in the air or in the soil.
– No harm to humans or pets or other insects apart from the pest being controlled.

Disadvantages of biological control:
– Control can be slow at first, particularly if the pest has got a strong hold.
– Cannot easily be used except on plants growing under cover.
– Pesticides will kill predators. There usually needs to be a pesticide-free interval of 30 days before introducing any biological controls.
– It is usually a lot more expensive than traditional, chemical control.
– Some predators are very sensitive to temperature and humidity. Amateur gardeners cannot always provide optimum conditions – another reason for using these controls under cover.

Pests on plants grown undercover, in greenhouses or houseplants

Pest	Biological Control
Caterpillars (butterflies and moths only)	*Bacillus thuringiensis* (naturally occuring bacterium)
Vine Weevil	*Heterorhabditis megidis* (parasitic nematode)
	Steinernema feltiae (parasitic nematode)
Sciarid fly	*Steinernema feltiae* (parasitic nematode)
	Heterorhabditis megidis (parasitic nematode)
	Hypoaspis miles (predatory, burrowing mite)
Slugs	*Phasmarhabditis hermaphrodita* (parasitic nematode)
Aphids	*Aphidius matricariae* (parasitic wasp)
	Aphidoletes aphidimyza (predatory midge larva)
	Praon bicolor (parasitic wasp)
White fly	*Encarsia formosa* (parasitic wasp)
Spider mite	*Phytoseiulus persimilis* (parasitic mite)
	Typhlodromus pyri (predatory mite)

Slug

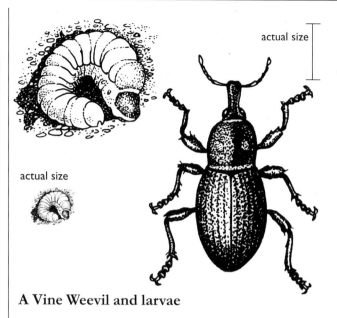

actual size

actual size

A Vine Weevil and larvae

ACTIVITY

A challenge!

– Record what pests you find and where and, if possible, how many.

– Record what beneficial creatures you find and where and how many.

– Experiment with protecting susceptible plants/crops from pests by several alternative methods. Record your success and identify which seem to be the most appropriate methods.

– Prevent ants, if you have them, from climbing up plants. They protect aphids from predators, such as ladybirds and lacewings, as they use the honeydew the aphids produce. When you have a foolproof ant deterrent or barrier – sell the rights. You'll make a fortune!

– Investigate methods of pest control from Victorian sources. Write to the RHS with a clear request: Royal Horticultural Society, PO Box 313, 80 Vincent Square, London SW1P 2PE (Tel. 0171 834 4333).

– What substance, in a slug trap, entices most slugs? (Try beer, milk, yoghurt.)

– How does time of year affect pest population?

– Does the weather affect some pests more than others?

– Why is yellow an important colour in the pest/predator world?

– Sow or plant varieties of plants known to be attractive to pests, and see what happens. *Fuchsia*, for instance, regularly suffers from white fly, so do tomatoes. Coleus, an ornamental houseplant, can be ruined by greenfly (aphid) attack.

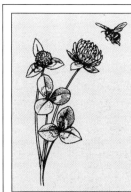

The Wildlife and Flower Garden

It is not difficult to establish a wildlife garden. If the conditions are right, wildlife will come to the garden, even if it is a strip one metre wide by ten metres long outside the reception class window, or a small corner at the end of the playground. Just as humans like a comfortable place to live, so do garden creatures. Give them the habitat they prefer and the food they need and they will move in. (See Plant Lists, pages 49–51.)

If there is space, why not have several small wildlife-attracting areas, as well as a designated 'wildlife garden', in your overall scheme. You could plant up corners for specific insects, such as butterflies or bees. You could allow an area of grass to grow long and seed – that will attract thousands of creatures. A smart sign can explain the purpose of each area, to avoid an accusation of untidiness!

What to plant

Small trees will not damage paths or foundations but will offer wildlife food and shelter. The dense foliage of shrubs will provide nesting sites for birds and many other small creatures and insects. Thick, low undergrowth will allow small mammals to move freely and find shelter. Plants and shrubs with berries will be excellent sources of food. If there is a wall available, plant shrubs which will 'hug' the wall. Bird boxes and feeding stations may also be fixed here, or on a fence. A mixture of flowers will entice many different creatures, including the important beneficial insects, whose food requirements include most garden pests (see page 30). An organic garden is attractive to wildlife – a wide range of careful planting provides an ideal habitat.

Section through a 1m wide x 10m long plot of 'wildlife' planting.

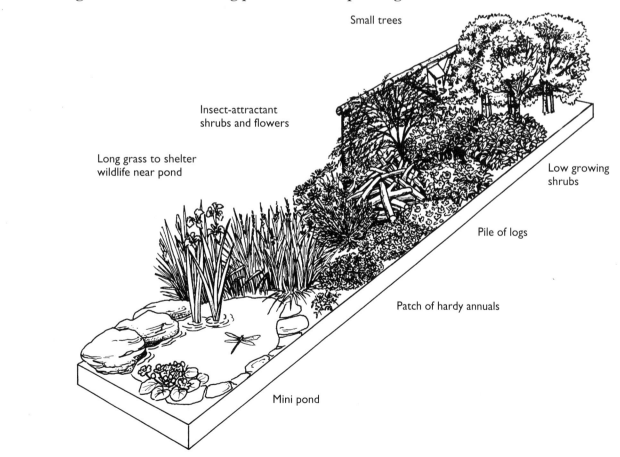

Small trees

Insect-attractant shrubs and flowers

Long grass to shelter wildlife near pond

Low growing shrubs

Pile of logs

Patch of hardy annuals

Mini pond

Preferred habitats for beneficial creatures (predators).

Predator	Where found	Over-winter
Ladybirds	wide range – hedgerows/ woodland/ grassland – found in and near colonies of aphids	in dead vegetation, under bark, in walls, under stones
Hoverflies	feed on pollen and nectar	in nooks and crannies
Lacewings	deciduous trees and shrubs – attracted by flowers (feed on nectar) and by sugary coating deposited on leaves by aphids	in nooks and crannies in gardens, sheds and houses
Ground beetles	live in soil and under mulches; feed at night	in obscure corners
Frogs & toads	Amphibians; frogs live in damp vegetation; toads prefer drier conditions	hibernate in obscure corners – under stones & plant debris
Anthocorids	in trees and shrubs	under bark; in hedgerows; in leaf litter
Birds	wherever there is food and shelter (including nesting boxes provided by humans)	in dense foliage of evergreen shrubs/trees

Food requirements for beneficials.

Insect	Food requirements
Ladybirds	aphids; pollen and nectar; other insects when aphids are scarce
Hoverflies	fruit tree spider mites; aphids (larvae); pollen & nectar (adults)
Lacewings	nectar (adults); aphids, mites, caterpillars (larvae)
Ground beetles	slugs, lettuce aphids, woodlice, root fly eggs & larvae, vine weevil larvae
Frogs & toads	slugs, snails, woodlice, ants
Anthocorids	aphids, capsid bugs, red spider mite, other pests of trees and shrubs
Birds	seeds, berries, insects and other creatures
Wasps	nectar, caterpillars and many other insects
Parasitic wasps and flies	caterpillars – many varieties
Hedgehogs	slugs and other insects
Spiders	wide range of insects
Centipedes	wide range of insects

Problems for beneficial creatures.

Beneficial creature	Problems
Ladybirds	all pesticides including Derris and insecticidal soaps
Hoverflies	all pesticides
Lacewings	all pesticides
Frogs & toads	fewer ponds and streams now; water pollution (garden ponds have become important habitats)
Anthocorids	all pesticides including organic ones
Ground beetles	slug bait and other pesticides
Parasitic wasps and flies	all pesticides including Derris
Wasps	become a nuisance in autumn and nests are destroyed
Birds	lack of food due to sprays killing off creatures they feed on
Spiders	all pesticides

Effects of pesticides

Pesticide residues can last a long time. If a school is surrounded by fields which are regularly sprayed with pesticides, or if the school fields are maintained with herbicides, it may be very difficult to provide uncontaminated ground in which beneficial creatures may thrive. If you are surrounded by open fields, find out if they are sprayed and, if they are, what they are sprayed with. Use the book 'U.K. Pesticide Guide' to obtain information about substances used.

All pesticides have to be registered by the Ministry of Agriculture, Fisheries and Food. Home-made mixtures are no longer permitted.

Caring for a wild life garden

Maintenance of a wildlife garden is usually very simple. It may be necessary to remove dead branches from shrubs or trees. Once the garden is established, there should be very little work. Add a mulch of compost or leaf-mould in the spring to areas where hardy annuals grow. There should be nothing added to a wildflower area – fertile soil will prevent flowering. Allow fallen leaves to lie and decompose naturally. A hedge or wall shrub may need clipping back. Roses need light pruning. Grass needs mowing.

Anthocorid bug

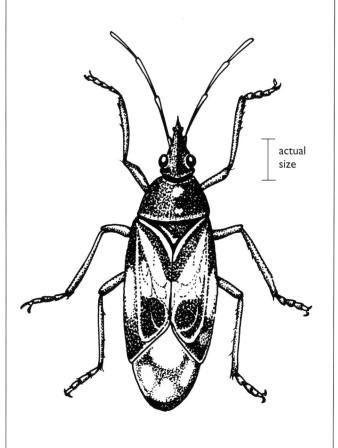

actual size

Check the school grounds, or a section of the school grounds:

- What plants – trees, shrubs, flowers – do you have already present, which are attractive to wildlife (see Plant Lists, pages 49–51)?
- What plants do you already have which are attractive to beneficial insects?
- Monitor the activity around these plants. What do you see? Can you identify the creatures?
- What is the earliest time in the year when you see pests? Beneficial insects?
- What is the latest time in the year when you see pests? Beneficial insects?

Check for any over-wintering insects in the school.

They can be found around window frames and behind blinds and curtains, in sheds and under sheltered parts of the outside of the school buildings.

Record different sorts of creatures and their habitats. Which creatures are found:

- Everywhere?
- Only in dark places?
- Only in light places?
- Only on vegetation?
- Only on the ground?
- Only in the ground?

Identify beneficial insects; identify pests.

- Find out which plants the pests will damage. Is there any difference between creatures found in the schools grounds and creatures found in other areas such as gardens and allotments? If there is a difference, what is it and why?

Investigate sprays used in the past.

The Royal Horticultural Society has useful records.

- If you have neighbours who spray, investigate what they are using and why.

If you can, set up a wildlife garden.

The area need not be large. There should be enough space for a range of plants to attract a reasonable variety of wildlife (see list at end of book). The finished area should be covered by planting, leaving no space for untidy weeds to grow, except in the area for hardy annuals. This can be mulched with leaf-mould in winter, to keep the soil protected and weed-free. Schools without open growing space may create a wildlife garden in tubs and other containers. A half-barrel will be adequate for a small tree and other pots may be used for shrubs and flowers.

- Measure the chosen site and plot it on a map.
- Parents' help could be enlisted to provide suitable plants.
- Prepare the ground; this work will depend on what has been on the site previously.
- Ground covering weeds should be cleared by a light-excluding mulch, or by hoeing.
- It is possible to plant through a mulch (see 'Ground clearing' and 'Weed control', page 9).
- Choose the correct wild flowers for your garden site and soil. There is a huge range to choose from. Wild flowers prefer poor soil. Trees and shrubs and herbaceous plants will need good soil in order to grow well.
- Make sure there are flowers all through the year as well as berries in winter, as a good food source.

Bring back butterflies

Narrow flower borders under windows are often boring strips filled with ground cover planting and a few roses. Why not turn them into glorious butterfly gardens? Choose some attractant shrubs and perennials as permanent plants, then each spring sow seeds of plants that will flower all summer. Select your plants with care, as food plants are not always the same ones needed for breeding. Lots of butterflies like grasses in which to lay their eggs. Many grasses are destroyed by weed killer, so butterflies are having difficulty in finding breeding sites. A butterfly border can provide pupils with the chance to watch the complete cycle of adult ... egg ... larva (caterpillar) ... chrysalis ... adult.

Did you know
1. One pair of blue-tits and their young will eat 10,000 caterpillars a year.
2. One hoverfly larva can eat up to 50 aphids a day, 1,000 in its lifetime.
3. Between 1990 and 1994 over 17,000 ponds were destroyed.
4. Over 400 spiders can be found per square metre in meadow land, in summer.
5. The larvae of ground and rove beetles will eat New Zealand Flatworm.

CHAPTER NINE

The Vegetable Garden

Many schools will already have a wildlife or conservation area. Establishing an area where vegetable gardening can take place will extend the range of available organic activities in a way that is usually popular with both staff and pupils. There may be some local organically-run allotments, whose owners would be a useful source of information if you contacted them. If you have no large area for vegetables, they can still be grown in small batches, or in pots (see list of suitable varieties on page 52). Wildflowers and vegetables can grow happily side by side!

Site

The choice of site requires careful consideration. An ideal site should have an open aspect, not over-shadowed by trees or tall buildings. The soil should not be water-logged at any time of the year, and areas near busy roads are inadvisable. They are frequently polluted because of traffic. In winter they often suffer salt contamination.

Vegetables prefer a sheltered growing area. If it is

Vegetables growing in a small plot.

Species suitable for screening and shelter, with advantages for wildlife.

Species	Wildlife (popular with.....)
Hornbeam (*Carpinus betulus*)	Nesting sites for birds
Oak (*Quercus spp*)	Acorns are food for a wide range of wildlife; supports 284 different insect species
Beech (*Fagus sylvatica*)	Pollen for bees; seeds for birds and small mammals; nesting sites for birds
Hawthorn (*Crataegus monogyna*)	Nectar; hips good for thrushes
Holly (*Ilex aquifolium*)	Berries for birds; nesting sites; nectar for bees
Hazel (*Corylus avellana*)	Nuts – a good food source
Dog Rose (*Rosa canina*)	Hips for birds; nesting sites for birds

windy, some sort of windbreak will be necessary. An immediate solution is plastic mesh fixed to wooden posts. However, this is expensive and easily vandalised. A hedge may be a long term solution, but it has several advantages. It is more attractive than a mesh fence. A mixture of species such as hawthorn (*Crataegus*), beech (*Fagus*), guelder rose (*Viburnum*) and holly (*Ilex*) will provide an ideal habitat for a wide range of beneficial wildlife. Fast growing shrubs, such as *Escallonia* or *Mahonia*, will shelter a small area very successfully.

Fast-growing *Leylandii* cypress is not an ideal plant although many people regard it as convenient. It soon reaches the required height, but then must be constantly kept in check. It can easily reach 30m. In addition it is not a native tree and consequently is not as good a source of food and shelter for native animals and insect species. Solid fencing should be avoided. As wind hits a fence it is thrown up and over the obstacle, resulting in turbulence on the 'sheltered' side. This can be very damaging to anything growing nearby.

Trees and shrubs tolerant of traffic pollution.

Trees	Shrubs	
Acer (*Acer*)	*Buddleia*	*Philadelphus*
Birch (*Betula*)	*Ceanothus*	*Ribes*
Hawthorn (*Crataegus*)	*Cornus*	*Sambucus*
Rowan (*Sorbus*)	*Forsythia*	*Weigela*
Willow (*Salix*)	*Hydrangea*	*Viburnum*
	Syringa	

Good sites:
– sunny
– sheltered
– near school
– away from roads
– good soil structure.

Sites to avoid:
– shadowed sites
– water-logged sites
– near road
– too far from school
– walls/fencing creating wind turbulence.

Wind turbulence caused by fencing.

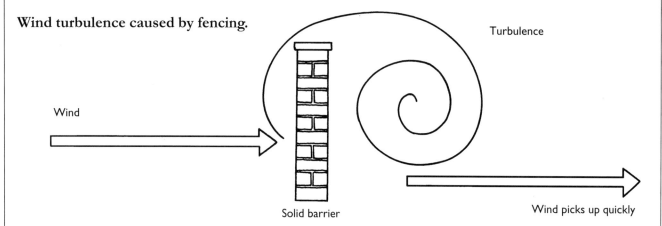

A shelter belt composed of a variety of growing shrubs and small trees diffuses the wind and reduces its strength for a distance equal to ten times the height of the hedge.

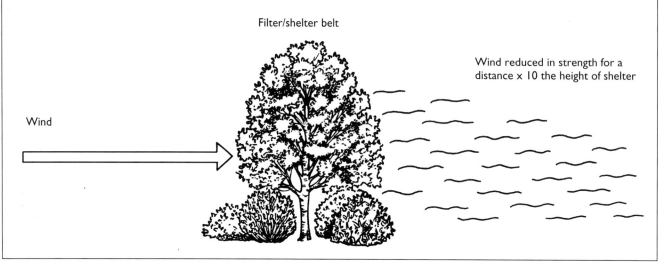

Choosing the vegetables

In order for pupils to benefit from growing vegetables, care must be taken in choosing the crop varieties. They must either be grown within a school year, i.e. harvested by mid-July, or they must survive the summer holidays and be ready for harvest in early September.

Crops which can be sown/planted and harvested in a school year include:
- radish
- spring onions
- courgettes
- early potatoes
- onions (autumn sown)
- early sown peas
- lettuce
- spinach (winter)
- cauliflowers

Crops which can survive the summer holidays (hopefully with a little assistance from pupils and parents or the caretaker) include:
- brassicas
- leeks
- root crops, if mulched
- main crop potatoes
- pumpkins
- beans for drying

Another factor in the choice of vegetables is the type of soil on the plot. While it is possible to grow most vegetables in all soil types, some vegetables prefer some soil types to others.

Vegetable	Clay	Sand
brassicas	✔	
carrots		✔
radishes		✔
potatoes	✔	
peas		✔

If possible, when choosing vegetable varieties, select those listed as being disease resistant. There is a good range now available and these are clearly identified in seed catalogues. For example:

Variety	Resistant to ...
Courgette: Supremo & Defender	Mosaic Virus
Leek: Autumn Mammoth	Rust
Lettuce: Beatrice & Avoncrisp	Root aphid & mildew
Potato: Cara & Kondor	Blight
Pea: Sugar Gem	Powdery mildew

Schools in the more northerly parts of the country may find it helpful to consult local allotment growers about which vegetable varieties succeed in the area. Temperature and light differences will affect growth quite considerably. Sun-loving crops such as tomatoes and sweet corn may not be successful in Northern England and Scotland.

Vegetable garden layout

It is better not to walk on growing areas. This compacts the soil and damages its structure. Consider a 'bed' system. Growing areas are one metre wide, with paths either side. The width makes it possible to reach from either side successfully, without stepping on the soil. The length of the bed is chosen for ease of movement around the garden. Always line the beds up so that they run from north to south, so that they have the sun on them all day.

The whole bed receives sunshine.

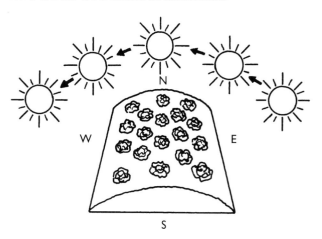

The plants on one side of the bed will tend to shade the other side.

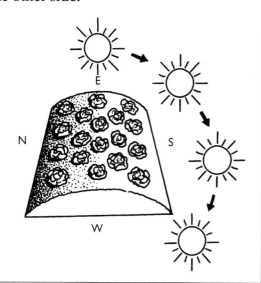

Although space is apparently lost in paths, the improved soil structure allows denser planting and there is little reduction in the quantity of crops produced. For younger children, a bed system can look more manageable. Work may easily be done from the paths.

No-dig

If, for any reason, digging is a problem, consider a 'no-dig' system. It is also very good for the soil. Literally, the area is never dug. Unwanted growth is cleared by a mulch. Again, it is possible to plant through this to get things going. Subsequent weeds are lightly hoed. The soil is covered with garden compost and this is taken down into the soil by the creatures within it. Potatoes can be laid on the surface and grown there, under a heavy mulch of hay. However, seed potatoes are susceptible to frost damage and it is better to put them in small holes before covering them. The holes can be made with a bulb planter or trowel. Then the area should be heavily mulched (15cm) with hay, under which the potato tubers develop. Other crops are sown in the normal way, disturbing the soil only slightly when the shallow drills are made for the seeds. The soil is always protected by a mulch or a crop of green manure (see page 12) if no crops are growing. When disposing of this, hoe it off and put it in the compost bin.

Rotation of crops in the vegetable garden

Crop rotation has been practised for hundreds of years. Until recently, it was an important method of pest and disease control for all gardeners and farmers. The idea is quite logical. If a crop is grown continuously on the same site over a period of years, the pests and diseases which favour that crop family will be able to establish themselves in the soil of the growing area. With a regular source of nourishment, it is not surprising that pests will multiply and diseases flourish.

On the other hand, if there is an annual change on a cyclical basis (rotation) of the growing sites in the vegetable garden, there is less chance for pests and diseases to build up and get out of control. When the larva of the Pea Moth drops to the ground in autumn to pupate and over-winter in the soil surrounding the peas, it fully expects to find a food source available the following spring. The adult emerges ready to feed, but the required food is no longer nearby. By the time the moths have located the new pea crop, a considerable number have succumbed to the birds, weather and beneficial insects.

There are of course a few problems, such as eelworm in potatoes, white rot in onions and clubroot in brassicas, which are persistent. Should your plot be infested by one of the long-term 'nasties' it is better to avoid growing the susceptible crop. The rotation time can be as long as 20 years before the pest or the spores die down!

Rotation is also a method of maintaining a balance of nutrients in the soil. Plants have specific needs as far as food is concerned. They each extract what they require during the growing season. If this demand is unaltered over a period of time, the nutritional balance of the soil will suffer.

Rotation of crops = pest and disease control

+

soil nutrition balance

A system has been devised which groups certain crops together, and moves them around from section to section over a period of at least four years. The requirements of each crop family follow on, and link into the preceding crop. This system of rotation is shown below.

A useful rotation in a vegetable garden is:

Plot	1st year	2nd year	3rd year	4th year
A	Roots	Potatoes	Onions & Legumes	Brassicas
B	Brassicas	Roots	Potatoes	Onions & Legumes
C	Onions & Legumes	Brassicas	Roots	Potatoes
D	Potatoes	Onions & Legumes	Brassicas	Roots

Crop family list:

Roots	Brassicas	Onions & Legumes	Potatoes
carrots parsnip	cabbage cauliflower Brussels sprouts broccoli calabrese wallflowers mustard turnips swede	onions leeks garlic shallots	

Other crops outside the main crop families can be grown alongside the rotational crops to fill in the gaps. Insect-attractant herbs, flowers, and small shrubs should also be grown wherever possible. The beneficial insects and birds they attract will assist in natural pest control. Ladybirds and their larvae will clean up an aphid infested plant quickly, but they have to be enticed to it in the first place. Birds will devour hundreds of caterpillars in summer, as well as over-wintering eggs if they are tempted in with seedheads such as sunflowers, and teasels. A well-balanced growing environment is what we are aiming for.

Thus, an allotment one year may well look like the first of the two diagrams below:

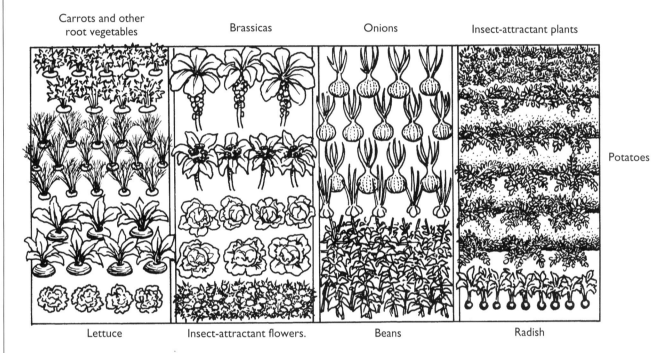

Carrots and other root vegetables   Brassicas   Onions   Insect-attractant plants

Potatoes

Lettuce   Insect-attractant flowers.   Beans   Radish

The following year the crops and some of the flowers have rotated, but the shrubs remain in situ.

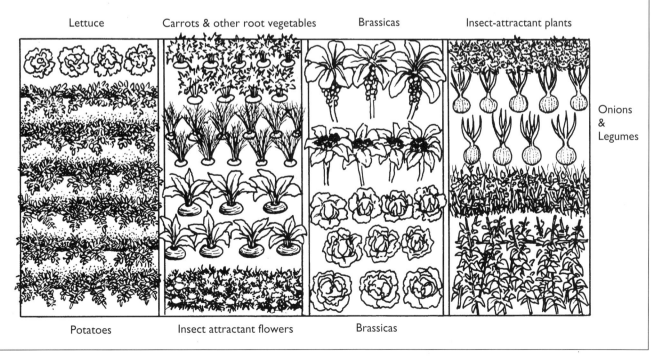

Lettuce   Carrots & other root vegetables   Brassicas   Insect-attractant plants

Onions & Legumes

Potatoes   Insect attractant flowers   Brassicas

A well-planned vegetable garden.

ACTIVITY

Set up and run a vegetable garden. Planning and preparation will be needed. Small garden tools can be used. All the garden skills, except heavy digging, will be needed.

Choosing a site:
– Survey the proposed site or sites.
– Prepare a plan of the area.
– Find out what the soil is, heavy/light/medium.
– Find out what the pH of the soil is.
– Check the area in all types of weather.
– Does frost stay in that ground for a long time (find out about 'frost pockets')?
– What is growing there now?
– How soon can it be cleared (see 'Ground clearing and weed control' section)?

A 'bed' system would enable several different classes each to have 'their' bed. Rotation would enable them to gain experience in a range of crops. They should:
– Take careful note of what crops were sown when and where.
– Note productivity.
– Compare findings annually.

– Take weather readings.
– Compare the relationship of crop productivity with weather conditions.
– Visit local allotments to observe rotation in practice.

Try one area as 'no-dig' to compare productivity. Remember, rotation has to be maintained in all areas.

Heavy spring rain can often batter newly germinated seedlings into the ground. Consider starting vegetables off inside and plant them out when they are sturdy young plants, and more tolerant of slightly adverse weather conditions. Sow some seeds directly into the ground too. Compare which plants do better during the growing season.

Did you know
1. As long ago as 1690, schools were advised to set up gardens. By 1914, there were at least 2,000 nation-wide.
2. During World War Two, school children often grew vegetables. One school grew 200 cauliflower, 300 broccoli, 400 leeks, 200 Brussels sprouts, and 1,000 cabbages in one season.

CHAPTER TEN
Water in the Organic Garden

In an ideal world, every school would have a pond large enough for half a class to work around simultaneously and deep enough to provide pond-dipping facilities. Few schools, however, are fortunate enough to have such a feature. Amongst other reasons, cost and safety are major factors against such installations. Nonetheless, water is very important in any garden and certainly so in organic gardening, where the wildlife attracted by a pond assists in pest control. A small pond is a way of providing the right habitat for these predators, whilst avoiding both excessive expenditure and danger zones. Pupils themselves are capable of constructing a small pond (or several if you have the space), as well as undertaking subsequent care and maintenance.

For the school with no ground to dig in, the solution may be a mini pond in a barrel or old

Beneficial creatures attracted by water	Pests controlled
Frogs and Toads	Slugs, woodlice, snails, ants
Hedgehogs	Slugs and lots of insects
Birds	Wide range of pests e.g. aphids, leather jackets, cutworm

basin. This system is quite capable of supporting some water creatures – even frogs, if you give them the right conditions. (See illustration on page 40.) There are many excellent books explaining in detail the many different ways in which a small pond can be constructed. This section contains a summary of some of these ways.

Cross-section for pond construction.

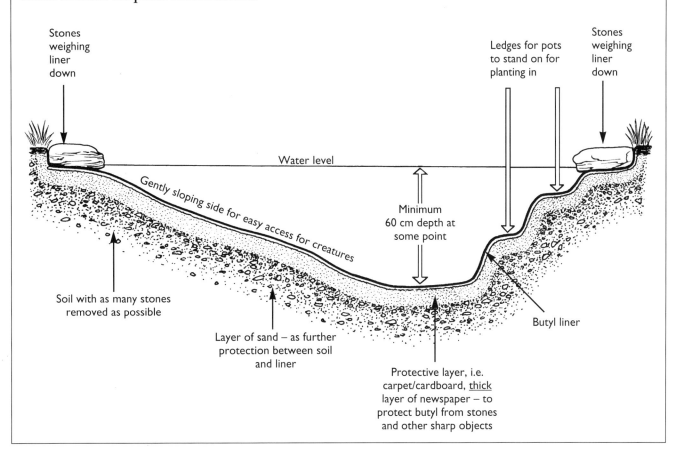

Stones weighing liner down

Ledges for pots to stand on for planting in

Stones weighing liner down

Water level

Gently sloping side for easy access for creatures

Minimum 60 cm depth at some point

Soil with as many stones removed as possible

Butyl liner

Layer of sand – as further protection between soil and liner

Protective layer, i.e. carpet/cardboard, thick layer of newspaper – to protect butyl from stones and other sharp objects

A pond must be:
– Completely water-tight.
– Deep enough to protect the creatures it contains.
– Constructed to allow birds, frogs and other creatures to use it easily.
– Sited to provide a comfortable growing/living environment for plant and animal life.
– Maintained regularly and carefully, particularly if it is small, to prevent the build-up of debris.

Dimensions

Although the length and width is optional, the one measurement crucial in a pond is depth. There must be a point at which this measures at least 60 cm. This enables pond-living creatures to survive freezing winter temperatures. Shallower ponds will not provide adequate protection, and in fact can freeze solid in winter or dry up in really hot summers.

Construction

As well as a minimum depth, your pond needs a shallow area and a sloping side which enables birds to bathe, hedgehogs to drink, and amphibians (frogs, toads, newts) to come and go freely. Vertical sides will prevent creatures from taking full advantage of this water and inhibit the use of the pond by the very creatures you are trying to attract. See illustration on page 39 for pond construction drawing

Site

The pond (or barrel) should be in an open, sunny site, although some shade is tolerated by plants and creatures. Avoid a position near trees, as falling leaves entering the water will decompose and turn the water sour. Ideally, the water should be visible from classroom windows, to allow creature-spotting from a useful 'hide'. There should be some planting around the edges, providing shelter for creatures coming and going.

 SAFETY NOTE

If the pond is in an out-of-the-way corner, a mesh covering should be considered, to prevent small children getting into difficulties.

Pond in a barrel.

Stones for amphibians to reach ground

Board to give exit ramp for amphibians

Plants in pots on bricks

Section through pond in a barrel.

Care and maintenance

An overhaul is best undertaken in the early autumn, before water creatures start to hibernate but after the summer breeding season. Any dead leaves should be removed, abundant plant growth should be reduced and excess waste should be removed from the bottom of the pond (leaving a little to provide living quarters). It is better to leave all material which has been taken out by the edge for a few days. Frequently there will be creatures enmeshed in the vegetation and they will then be able to return to the water and find a new corner in which to live.

As this is an organic garden, there will of course be no harmful sprays which can kill pond life. A major problem in recent years has been run-off into waterways of pesticides and herbicides. Water-dwelling creatures have been killed as a consequence.

Research
– See how many readily-available garden products state 'Dangerous to fish' or 'Keep away from ponds'.

In the spring, be sure to remove waste, including leaves that may have fallen into the pond since the autumn clean up. As the water warms up, waste material can start to decompose, thereby upsetting the pond balance. It might be useful to change some of the water at this time – about 10%. Certainly, if the level is down, a top-up is essential. If you have spawn in the pond, remember to provide, if necessary, an exit ramp for the emerging amphibians. This is particularly important when the pond is in a barrel.

Materials to line a pond

Probably the best material for a small pond in a school garden would be a heavy duty butyl rubber liner. This pond liner comes in various sizes according to the pond dimensions required, and can be shaped in any way, although sharp corners are difficult. (See Activity)

The alternatives are:
– Pre-shaped fibreglass shells (with limited choice of shape and size).
– Black polythene sheeting (which has a fairly short life).
– Concrete (which is usually too costly, and not really practical for a mini-pond).

Butyl enables the pond-makers to have any shape they like and to slope the sides gently, providing the necessary requirements for the range of wildlife mentioned earlier. The liner needs protection from sharp stones in the soil around and underneath it. A layer of old carpet is ideal, although a thick layer of sand and/or cardboard or newspaper can be adequate.

Making a butyl-lined pond

– Dig the hole (see Activity for measurements); remember to allow enough depth. The protective layer will take up space.
– Make sure the rim of the pond is level, using a spirit level.
– Clear out all sharp stones on or near the surface.
– Put a 5 cm layer of sand all over the pond base and sides.
– Place protective layer of old carpet/cardboard in the hole, over the sand.
– Place butyl liner into pond, allowing an adequate overlap around the rim – 50 cm is good (the liner does not have to touch the pond bottom).
– Weight down the edges of the liner all round the pond rim with stones.

Well-developed small pond.

– Fill the pond with water (as the weight of the water increases, the liner will stretch to fit the hole you have prepared).
– It is all right to use mains tap water as any chlorine will dissipate naturally after a few days; the nutrients in the water will cause some problems, but this is not serious in the long term.
– Plant your plants; you can use plants in pots which stand on the bottom and on the ledges of the pond; you can put sieved, stone-free soil direct on the liner about 5cm deep and plant directly into it; or you can do a combination of the two.
– Cover spare liner material around the rim of the pond with extra stones, or bury it under the soil, so it is not in the light, which would cause the fabric to deteriorate.

Time-scale

There is no ideal time of year to start your pond. Whichever time of year you choose to begin, there will be advantages and disadvantages.

If you begin in the autumn term, by the time the essential planning stage is over, covering the measurements, design, and necessary preparation, the weather could well be against digging. Plants should not be planted now, and pond life is 'resting' during the winter months. Nonetheless, you could do the work, fill the pond, thereby allowing the water to lose its 'newness' and wait until the spring for the plants. You would also be ready for any frogs which may decide to lay spawn.

If you do the design work in the autumn, but wait for the spring for the practical work, you'll probably miss the frog spawn, although the following year you'll have a much more mature site, which could prove attractive. Also, the pond will be ready at the best time for planting.

	Jan.	Feb.	Mar.	Apr.	May	Jun.	Jul.	Aug.	Sept.	Oct.	Nov.	Dec.
Plants growing actively			●	●	●	●	●	●				
Plants dying back									●	●		
No plant growth	●	●									●	●
Pond life very active				●	●	●	●	●	●			
Pond life fairly active			●							●		
Pond life quiescent	●	●									●	●

There will of course be regional differences in the above time-table.

If you start everything in the summer, some pupils will leave before they see their work completed, but the pond will attract wildlife (possibly frogs) during the summer or early autumn, and there will be some plant growth. The decision is a difficult one for a school.

Birds will take advantage of a pond all year round. They need it for bathing and for drinking.

Plants for the pond

Even a small pond can have a fairly wide range of plants, providing these are chosen with care. You should try to have at least one floating plant, a deep-water plant, a shallow-water plant and a sub-merged plant in your mini-pond. The number required varies according to the pond size. This selection will give plenty of interest, as well as a good range of habitats for pond life. If you can arrange to have a 'boggy' area near the pond edge there are many plants which enjoy such conditions. (See Plant Lists, pages 49–51.)

⚠ WARNING ⚠

Avoid Canadian Pondweed (*Elodea candensis*) and Australian Swamp Stone Crop (*Crassula helmsii* or *Tillea recurva*). THEY TAKE OVER.

Submerged plants

– are not only home for small creatures, they aerate the water and contribute to the health of the pond. By using up waste nutrients in the water, they starve any algae growth and keep the water clear.

Floating plants

– provide cover, homes and shelter for pond life, and, by reducing light, reduce algae.

Shallow-water and deep-water plants

– all offer shelter and interest. It would be on their top growth that pupils could well see a dragonfly unfolding its wings for the first time.

Plants in perforated plastic pond baskets

– should be in heavy manure-free garden soil, and covered in washed gravel to keep the soil in place. Avoid peat-based fertilisers and composts, they cause a wide range of difficulties. If you are going to put a layer of soil directly onto the liner, use the same manure- and peat- free base.

Problems

Small ponds tend to have more problems than large ones, because there is not much space to absorb difficulties. Drying up in summer is an example. The pond will need regular topping up but, if you use mains water straight from the tap, the nutrients and chlorine will upset the pond balance. A solution is to have a reserve container, where water can be stored for a while before it is added to the depleted pond. Fill a container in the afternoon. Leave it in a shady corner to come up to air temperature – 24 hours is enough. This will allow chlorine to dissipate. Add the water to the pond the next afternoon. Re-fill the container ready for the following day. The long summer holidays will need some thought, of course.

Again, on the subject of nutrients, the 'green water' pond is in fact thick algae growth which is induced by the nutrients in mains tap water. The organically maintained garden will not be using artificial fertilisers which leach into the water, so once the floating and submerged plants have established themselves, and some algae-eaters (such as *Daphnia* [water fleas]) have arrived or been added, this green growth usually vanishes. Whatever happens, do not replace the water. This will just start the cycle again. The plant cover should be about one-third of the total surface of the pond. This combination of cover with plant and insect requirements is usually enough to control the algae.

The weed that looks like fine green hair is blanketweed. If this becomes a problem, remove with a stick. Remember to leave it near the pond for a couple of days to allow pond life to return to the water. It can then be put on the compost heap.

ACTIVITY

Pond-making

Start to plan:
- Survey possible areas.
- Decide on several possible sites.
- Discuss advantages and disadvantages for each site.
- Make a choice of site.
  (A pond in a barrel will present less physical demands, but will still require consideration of most of the above points. In addition, allowance will need to be made for amphibians, which pose a totally different design requirement from a pond in an open space.)

Measure the pond site and mark it out.

Work out the amount of pond liner required to fit the pond:
- Remember to allow for a generous overlap onto the soil surround (usual amount = (length +[depth x 2]) by (width +[depth x 2])).
- For a pond one metre long by 40cms wide allow (100 + [60 x 2]) by (40 + [60 x 2]) = 220 x 160 cm.

Plants

Find out which plants are 'aquatic' (deep water) and which are 'marginal' (shallow water):
- Where do they come from?
- Can all plants live with water at their roots? Permanently?

Soil

Examine the soil that is extracted from the pond site:
  (Pupils can dig out a small pond themselves using trowels.)
- Does it change colour lower down? What about texture?
- Check it for humus level (see reference to jam jar test on page 13).
- What living creatures are present in the soil? Are they 'good' or 'bad'?
- How much soil (weight) has been removed? (You may have to weigh a portion and estimate the whole.)
- Is the heap of soil the same size as the hole it came from? (It is usually bigger, due to the air it holds once dug.)
- Can this weight change for any reason? (Dry it out and re-weigh it.)

What are you going to do with the soil that you have removed?
- You could spread it out on an observable surface and see how many birds come to eat the soil-dwelling creatures.
- Which birds come? How many?
- What are their feeding requirements?

Pond visitors and residents

Frogs are good to have in the organic garden:
- Will you wait and hope? Or will you get some spawn and introduce it?
- What conditions do frogs need?
- What will encourage frogs to lay spawn in a pond?
- What eats frog spawn?
- Why are garden ponds so important to the frog population nowadays?

Which birds visit to bathe and drink?
- What are their favourite foods?
- Will they help keep down pests?

CHAPTER ELEVEN

Window Sill Planting

It is very exciting to sow seeds in small pots, put them on a sunny window sill and watch them grow. Whether the plants remain in the classroom or are eventually transferred outside, pupils will have had the opportunity to watch the growing process from start to finish. Schools with no greenhouse will find window-sill planting an ideal way to get some plants growing before transplanting them to an outside area.

Pots or window-sill troughs of flowers and vegetables can be grown permanently in the classroom. Cucumbers, peppers and tomatoes will all do well inside in a sunny south-facing situation. They will need to be in large pots (30cm) if they are to produce crops. Assuming that windows are opened in the summer, there will probably be a few pests and diseases to overcome.

Types of plants

Half-hardy plants

– need to be germinated in warmth, and grown in warmth until frost danger is past. This usually means late May or early June.

Typical half-hardy plants:

Flowers	Food plants
Lobelia	Courgette
Nicotiana	Tomatoes
Dianthus	Peppers
Ageratum	Cucumbers
	Aubergine
	Pumpkins

Hardy plants

– may be germinated and grown outside. Some seedlings benefit from being grown in pots or trays under cover. A cold greenhouse is ideal but if that is not available, a cloche over the growing area is fine. Protection prevents young seedlings from being scratched up by animals and birds, or being beaten down by rain and wind.

Flowers	Food plants
Alyssum Sunflower Californian Poppy Baby Blue Eyes Straw flower Mignonette	Most of the common ones grown. Some benefit from being started indoors. You can produce sturdy plants which will stand up to adverse weather conditions. Runner Beans and French Beans for example.

Annual plants

– grow from a seed, set flower and fruit and then die in one growing season.

Perennial plants

– grow from a seed or cutting, set flower and fruit and continue season after season.

Biennial plants

– grow from a seed one season, over-winter, then set flower and fruit the second season, before dying.

Seeds and seedlings

To germinate, most seeds (not all) need warmth not light. It is not until the seedling leaves have appeared that a brightly lit situation is required. Once the leaves are through the surface of the growing medium, make sure the pots are on a sunny window sill. However, young seedlings can be scorched and withered by the full blast of the summer mid-day sun on a south-facing ledge. The white paint-on shading in greenhouses is designed to protect young plants from this problem. Similarly, protection in schools can be achieved by erecting a thin, plain white paper screen which is in place during the hottest time of the day. Obviously, this will not always be needed. A north-facing class-room will require no shading at all.

Shaded window sill.

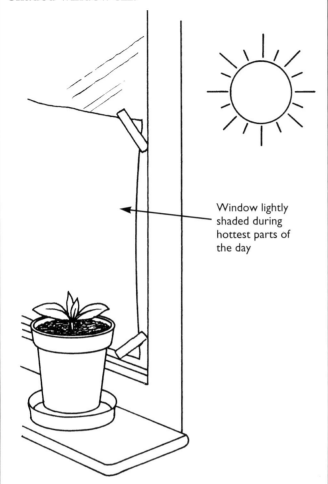

Window lightly shaded during hottest parts of the day

Sturdy young plant in good light.

Plant too far away from window to benefit from light, becoming 'drawn' and leggy.

Large seeds such as courgette and tomato can be sown singly; smaller seeds such as alyssum and chives can be sown in small clusters. Sow seeds in pots. At the appropriate time these pots of seedlings can be planted outside. Some seeds will not respond favourably to the warmth of a class-room. Polyanthus and pansies, for example, require cool conditions for successful germination. It is essential to abide by the requirements listed on the seed packet. It is not necessary to spend money on pots and trays. Most of these items can be made from recycled material.

Light requirements

After germination, pots of seedlings must be as close to a window as possible. The reduction in light values even 20cm from the glass will cause seedlings in the back row to become 'drawn', that is long and leggy, as opposed to sturdy plants.

A photographer's light meter will show different light values clearly. A solution is to fit a reflecting screen at the back of the plants. Light coming through the window will be reflected onto the rear of the plots and the plants will not 'lean'. A piece of kitchen foil fixed to card is quite adequate for this task.

The simplest way is to have two or three rows of pots in a waterproof container, which has a high back and a low front. This can be a plastic lined cardboard box, cut away to make a suitable tray.

The back of the container is covered in foil (see Activity).

The pots may remain in a container such as this from germination until transplanting time, providing their water and light requirements are adequately met.

Pots in waterproof container.

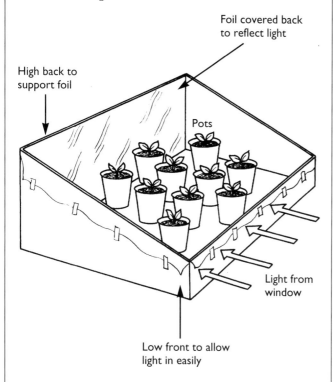

High back to support foil

Foil covered back to reflect light

Pots

Light from window

Low front to allow light in easily

Watering young plants

The growing medium the seedlings are in must be kept moist (not wet) at all times. Seedlings are sensitive to dryness at the roots. They have very fine root hairs. If these dry out the plant can die. A waterproof tray makes it possible for plants to be watered easily, by pouring water into the tray (see Activity). Alternatively, using a watering can with a very fine rose, water the seedlings from above. Take care not to do this if the sun is shining on the young plants. They will become scorched due to the strong light shining through water droplets on the delicate leaves.

Growing media

Avoid peat-based growing media. The destruction of peat-bogs has become very serious in recent years. Plants and creatures which depend on the bogs for survival have fewer and fewer sites in which to live. Peat is a finite resource which must be guarded carefully. There are many varieties of non-peat-based growing media available now.

Hardening off

When the time is right, transfer young plants to their outside growing site. The plants can be left in their paper pots. These will break down in the soil naturally.

Some plants need to be introduced to the outside world carefully – 'hardened off'. This entails putting them outside during the day but bringing them in at night for about a week. Then leave them out but cover them over at night with paper or plastic again for a week. Then they can be planted outside. This process is usually used for plants which originate in warmer countries such as Spain, Italy or Southern France. Most of these plants are 'half-hardy'. Some examples of half-hardy flowers and food plants are listed on page 44.

Common indoor pests

Aphids flourish in the warmth and relative stillness indoors and here they are difficult to control with beneficial insects. These do not willingly fly inside, whereas the aphids are wafted in on air currents. Select flowers (see Plant List, pages 50–51) which will attract beneficial insects, such as lacewings, hover flies and ladybirds, but you may need to remove aphids by hand.

Red Spider Mite is another common indoor plant pest. The mites are usually found on the underside of leaves, where they create fine 'webs'. They feed by sucking the juices from the plant. The leaves begin to look blotchy and finely mottled. If this pest is not controlled, the leaves will be sucked dry and fall, and there will just be bare stems left. There is a biological control to combat this pest, the predatory mite *Phytosieulis persimilis*. This may be purchased from various sources. It is introduced to affected plants, where it devours the red spider mites. There is no danger that it will take over the role of pest. Once its food source is gone, it will die out naturally. It is quite harmless to everything except the spider mite.

Soft Scale and Mealy Bug are two more pests that can damage plants grown indoors. Soft Scale looks like small brown lumps. It is usually found along the central veins of leaves but in a bad infestation it can be everywhere. Mealy Bug looks like small lumps of fluffy cotton, tucked into cracks and joints. Cactus plants often have Mealy Bug around the prickles! Both these pests can be removed with toothpicks. Just scrape them off, without damaging the plant.

Recycling

Make paper plant pots for seed sowing:

- Using newspaper (black and white printing only), roll a sheet around a tube, such as a wooden rolling pin or a DIY mastic tube.
- Slide carefully off tube.
- Staple at each end of roll.
- Cut into 8–10cm lengths, stapling at one end of each length to hold the 'pot' together.

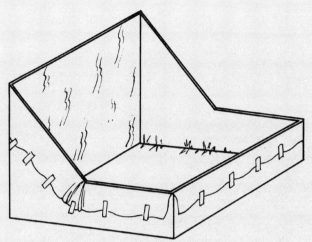

Side view of cardboard box prepared to accept seedlings. Line with plastic. Cover back with reflective foil, to direct light onto rear of plants and reduce 'leaning' towards light.

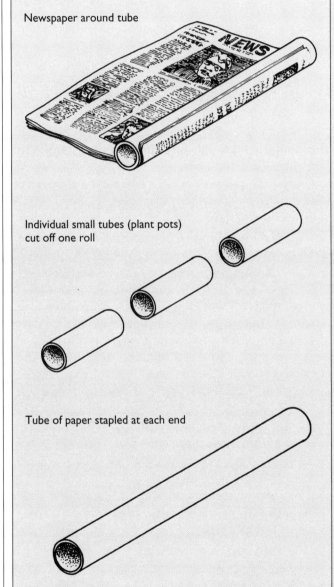

Newspaper around tube

Individual small tubes (plant pots) cut off one roll

Tube of paper stapled at each end

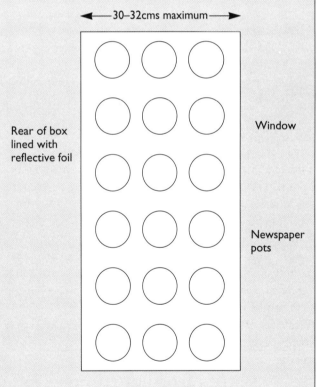

◄—— 30–32cms maximum ——►

Rear of box lined with reflective foil

Window

Newspaper pots

Place pots in container, no more than three rows deep.

What else can be used to make plant containers?

Make containers for holding the plant pots:

- Take a cardboard box which will easily fit on the ledge. Cut out front to leave only 3–4cm height. Cut away most of the sides for about two-thirds of their length, then angle up to leave a high back. Line base and sides with plastic. Line back with reflective cooking foil.

Try out different growing media with the same plants:

- Use a peat-free organic growing medium. There is quite a wide choice now available.

- Alternatively, you could use finely-sieved garden soil. Mix it with leaf-mould or garden compost to improve texture and fertility.
- Observe carefully which seedlings and which growing media are most successful.

Using long planting troughs:
- (Use plastic ones, available commercially, with a drip tray), grow a range of plants specifically to attract insects.
- What do you entice into the classroom? Friend or foe?
- If you have a suitable site indoors, try growing different crops in 'growing-bags' or large (30cm) pots.
- Plants can be fed organically, with the liquid feed from nettles or comfrey, or with the products from a worm bin. In order to achieve a 'fair test', try out different feeds on plants which are otherwise grown in exactly the same conditions.

Investigate:
- What depends on peat bogs for survival? Plants? Creatures?
- How much peat bog has been consumed?
- Why has peat become so popular in gardens?
- What can replace it?
- What is the pH of peat?
- Why does this pH make peat so useful?
- What happens to peat bogs when they have been stripped?
- Where are peat bogs found? In the UK? In Europe?
- What are the advantages of using a commercial growing medium (potting compost) instead of garden soil?
- What is the difference between garden soil and bought growing medium?
- What is 'loam'? What is 'John Innes' compost?

Plants from cuttings

It is possible to produce new plants from cuttings, as well as from seed. Sections of plant stem, cut from a growing plant, will root when inserted into an open, well-drained growing medium. Many interior plants can be propagated in this way, so can plants which normally grow outside, but which require warmth in the early stages of root development. Pupils can care for these cuttings in the warmth of the classroom. When they have rooted, they can be 'hardened off' before being planted out in the school garden. This is an excellent, economical way of stocking a garden, as well as an ideal chance for pupils to experiment with different plants and different growing media.

An ideal time for this activity is May/June, when plants are growing strongly.

Taking cuttings:
- Choose a non-flowering, strongly-growing side shoot from this year's growth.
- Cut it off just below a leaf joint, about 10 cm from the tip of the shoot.
- Remove about one third of the leaves from this cutting. Leaves 'transpire' (sweat) and you have just deprived them of their only means of taking up water (through the roots).
- Insert the cutting into a pot of moist growing media. Coir has been found to be ideal for this purpose. Put 4 or 5 cuttings into a 8 cm pot.
- Place a plastic cover over the pot to prevent the cuttings from drying out. Use a bottle cloche made from the top half of a fizzy drinks bottle, with the cap removed. The few plants which should not be covered like this are *Pelargonium* (Geranium), cactus and succulents.
- When new growth is seen at the shoot tip, carefully lift the cuttings out and re-pot them singly into larger pots to grow on.
- Harden off if they are to be planted outside.

Tips for Success:
- All equipment should be scrupulously clean. Dirty pots can harbour fungal diseases.
- Cuttings lose moisture very quickly, so don't cut off too many at once – they will wilt.
- Place newly cut material into a pot of water to avoid moisture loss before potting.
- Once potted, keep the cuttings out of direct sunlight until they have rooted.
- Make sure the leaves of cuttings in a pot don't overlap; good air circulation is essential.
- Keep the growing medium just moist. If it is too wet, rotting can occur.
- Remove the bottle cloche every day for 5 minutes to allow fresh air around the cuttings.
- Try to keep an even temperature.

Some plants suitable for cuttings:
Berberis, Cotoneaster, Escallonia, Pelargonium (Geranium), *Cornus* (Dogwood), *Ribes* (Flowering Currant), *Forsythia.*

Plant Lists

Trees, shrubs and other plants to attract wildlife

	Birds		Bees		Butterflies		Other Insects	
	food	shelter	food	shelter	food	shelter	food	shelter
TREES								
Beech (*Fagus sylvatica*) (use as hedge)	●						●	●
Birch (*Betula pendula*) (grow small variety)	●						●	●
Crab Apple (*Malus sylvestris*)	●						●	●
Hazel (*Corylus avellana*)	●							
Holly (*Ilex aquilfolium*)	●	●	●		●	●		
Lilac (*Syringa*)	●		●		●		●	
Oak (*Quercus*) (grow as hedge)	●	●			●	●	●	●
Prunus spp (many varieties possible)	●		●		●		●	●
Rowan (*Sorbus aucuparia*)	●		●		●		●	●
Wayfaring Tree (*Viburnum lantana*)	●		●		●		●	
SHRUBS								
Berberis (*Berberis spp*)	●		●				●	
Bridal Wreath (*Spirea arguta*)			●					
Butterfly bush (*Buddleia spp*)	●		●		●		●	
Cotoneaster (*Cotoneaster spp*)	●		●				●	
Escallonia (*Escallonia spp*)			●		●		●	
Firethorn (*Pyracantha*) (very thorny; grow as wall shrub)	●	●	●		●		●	

	Birds		Bees		Butterflies		Other Insects	
	food	shelter	food	shelter	food	shelter	food	shelter
Flowering Currant (*Ribes sanguineum*)			●		●			
Hypericum (*Hypericum* 'Hidcote', NOT *H. calycinum*)	●		●		●		●	
Honeysuckle (climber) (*Lonicera spp*)		●	●		●	●	●	●
Lavender (*Lavendula*)			●		●			
Potentilla (*Potentilla spp*)			●		●		●	
Quince (*Chaenomeles japonica*)	●		●					
Rosemary (*Rosmarinus officinalis*)								
Skimmia (*Skimmia japonica*)	●						●	
Snowy Mespilus (*Amelanchier lamarckii*)			●		●			
Viburnum (many varieties esp. winter flowering ones)	●		●				●	
HERBS								
Borage (*Borago officinalis*)			●		●		●	
Chives (*Allium schoenoprasum*)			●		●		●	
Fennel (*Foeniculum vulgare*)			●				●	
Feverfew (*Tanacetum parthenium*)			●				●	
Marjoram (*Origanum vulgare*)			●		●		●	
Thyme (*Thymus spp*)			●		●		●	
ANNUALS & BIENNIALS								
California Poppy (*Eschscholzia*)			●		●		●	
Candytuft (*Iberis umbellata*)			●		●		●	

	Birds		Bees		Butterflies		Other Insects	
	food	shelter	food	shelter	food	shelter	food	shelter
Cornflower (*Centaurea spp*)			●		●		●	
Forget-me-not (*Myosotis*)			●		●		●	
Marigold (*Calendular officinalis*)			●		●		●	
Mignonette (*Reseda odorata*)			●		●		●	
Straw flower (*Helichrysum bracteatum*)			●		●		●	
Sunflower (*Helianthus annuus*)	●		●		●		●	
Tobacco plant (*Nicotiana*)			●		●		●	
White Alyssum (*Lobularia maritima*)			●		●		●	

Herbaceous plants for nectar or seed

Catmint (*Nepeta spp*)

Christmas rose (*Helleborus spp*)

Golden Rod (*Solidago*)

Honesty (*Lunaria annua*)

Ice plant (*Sedum spectabile*)

Leopards Bane (*Doronicum plantagineum*)

Perennial cornflower (*Centaurea dealbata*)

Phlox (*Phlox spp*)

Poached egg plant (*Limnanthes douglasii*)

Polyanthus (*Primula variabilis*)

Scabious (*Scabiosa spp*)

Spring Crocus (*Crocus spp*)

Wallflower (*Cheiranthus cheiri*)

Plants for ponds

Deep water aquatics
– Water Lillies (*Nymphaea spp*). Choose the correct size for your pond. Vigorous lilies can take over a small pond. Check the final spread before buying.

Floating plants
– eg Water Soldier (*Stratiotes aloides*). Looks like a pineapple top. Again, check for over-vigorous growth when selecting from this group.

Oxygenators (Submerged plants)
– These important plants help keep the water free of algae. They also provide the pond's oxygen supply. eg. *Ranunculus spp*.

Shallow water or emergent plants
– These have their roots submerged but their foliage and flowers in the air. The depth of planting depends on the plant. Choose the one for your pond according to the situation. eg. *Caltha spp, Typha spp, Iris spp*.

Vegetables to grow in containers

	Varieties	Planting details
Bean, French	Purple Tepee/Kinghorn Wax/Pros Gitana	4 plants per 10 litre pot
Carrot	any early variety, eg. Early Nantes	plant 4cm apart in the pot
Chard	Lucullus (white stems) or Ruby (red stems)	plant 1 per 4 litre pot
Courgette	Ambassador/Early gem/Gold Rush	plant 1 per 30 litre pot
Cucumber	Bush Crop/Burpless Tasty Green	plant 1 per 30 litre pot
Leek	King Richard	plant 4cm apart
Lettuce	choose for taste	for large varieties plant 1 per 4 litre pot; for small size, plant 2–3 per 4 litre pot.
Onion	any variety from sets	7.5cm – 10cm apart
Pea	Kelvedon Wonder	plant 8 per 10 litre pot
Pepper	Redskin	plant 1 per 10 litre pot
Potato	early varieties only, eg. Maris Bard/ Pentland Javelin	Use lidless dustbin. Remember to make drainage holes in bottom of bin. Place 10cm layer rich soil on base. Lie seed potatoes on top. Cover with soil. As tops begin to grow through, add more soil, until the level of the soil is 3cm below the top of the bin. Do not allow to dry out. Support bin on blocks. In a normal size dustbin, plant 5 seed potatoes.
Radish	any	Sow 2.5cm apart
Tomato	Pixie/Totem/Tumbler	plant 1 per 15 litre pot

Glossary of gardening terms

Compost
Mixture of garden, kitchen and household waste which when decomposed may be used in the garden.

Frost Pocket
Area of a garden where, in frosty weather, the soil remains cold and may not be free of frost through-out the day. A danger zone for tender plants.

Growing Medium
The substance that plants grow in. A term particu-larly used when talking about plants grown in con-tainers. Growing media may be peat-based, or soil-based, or based on another main ingredient. It will have added to it the required plant nutrients. These may be artificially manufactured, or of organic origin.

Herbicide
Poison which kills plants.

Mulch
Covering, over soil or around plants, to hold in moisture, exclude light or feed plants.

Pesticide
Poison which kills insects.

Rotation
Moving plants, particularly vegetables, around the site or within the garden over a period of 3, 4 or 5 years to avoid a build up of pests and disease and to reduce the loss of soil nutrients.

Rotavate
Dig over the ground using a machine.

Soil structure
The way individual particles of soil are bound together.

Useful Reading

Beds
Pauline Pears
HDRA & Search Press

Beekeeping
Dr John Feltwell
LTL/Southgate

Butterflies
Dr John Feltwell
LTL/Southgate

From the **'EXPERT'** series
Dr D G Hessayon
The Garden Expert
The Tree & Shrub Expert
The Flower Expert
(Although the 'Expert' series is not organic, the information contained is clear and very easy to use by those whose gardening knowledge is minimal or even non-existent.
PBI Publications

Fundraising for School Grounds
W Lucas & Anne Mountfield
LTL/Southgate

Garden Creepy Crawlies
Michael Chinery
Whittet Books

Gardening for Butterflies
British Butterflies Conservation Society

Garden Plants Valuable to Bees
International Bee Research Association
Whittet Books

Greenhouses
Sue Stickland
HDRA & Search Press

Healthy Fruit & Vegetables
Pauline Pears & Bob Sherman
HDRA & Search Press

How to Make a Wildlife Garden
Chris Baines
Elm Tree Books

How to Make your Garden Fertile
Pauline Pears
HDRA & Search Press

Land and Water Invertebrates
Lynette Merrick
LTL/Southgate

Living Garden, The
Michael Chinery
Dorling Kindersley

Organic Gardening
Edited by Geoff Hamilton
Dorling Kindersley

People, Plants and Places
Julian Agyeman
LTL/Southgate

Pest Control
Pauline Pears & Bob Sherman
HDRA & Search Press

Pond Design Guide
Graham Flatt
LTL/Southgate

Pondwatch Factsheets 1, 2 & 3
The Wildfowl & Wetlands Trust
(Slimbridge)
Wildfowl and Wetlands Trust

Recycling – A Practical Guide for the School Environment
Dr John Feltwell
LTL/Southgate

School Grounds Resource Directory
LTL
LTL/Southgate

Science in the School Grounds
Gill Thomas
LTL/Southgate

Simple Guide to Organic Gardening
Bob Sherman
Collins & Brown

Slugs, Snails and Earthworms
Dr John Feltwell
LTL/Southgate

Soil Care
Jo Readman
HDRA & Search Press

Starting a Wildlife Pond
Peter Sibley
School Garden Company

Step by Step information leaflets:
Composting
Gardening for Wildlife
Gardening with Beneficial Insects for Natural Pest Control
Gardening with Green Manures
On the Slug Trail
Pest Control Without Poisons
Starting an Allotment
Weed Control Without Chemicals
What is Organic Gardening?
Why Garden Organically?
Worm Composting
HDRA
Ryton Organic Gardens
Ryton-on-Dunsmore
Coventry
CV8 3LG

Trees in the School Grounds
Rosemary Clark & Peter Walters
LTL/Southgate

Wildlife Gardening
Fran Hill
Derbyshire Wildlife Trust

Wildlife and the School Environment
RSPB/LTL
LTL/Southgate

POSTERS:
Making the Best of your School Grounds
LTL/Southgate

Learning Outdoors
LTL/Southgate

VIDEOS:
Grounds for Celebration
Presented by Sir David Attenborough
LTL/Southgate

Making the Best of Your School Grounds
LTL/Southgate

For further information about organic gardening, contact The Henry Doubleday Research Association

The Henry Doubleday Research Association (HDRA) is Britain's leading organic gardening organization. Its main base is at Ryton Organic Gardens, on a 20 acre site where the demonstration gardens are open all year round to visitors. In April 1995 a second organic garden was opened at Yalding, near Maidstone.

The aim of the HDRA is to promote environmentally sound, organic growing techniques worldwide. The organic message is spread through books, leaflets, newspaper and magazine articles, as well as TV and radio.

The research facilities at Ryton enable staff to conduct a wide variety of trials. The aim is not to ignore modern developments but to see how best they can be used and adapted to an organic system. There has been considerable investigation into resistant varieties of vegetables and different types of organic peat-free growing media.

The Heritage Seed Library has been established to save old, unusual and outlawed vegetable varieties. Members of the Library have access to a range of seeds which are no longer commercially available.

The Third World Organic Support Group helps developing countries with tree seeds and seedlings selected for their usefulness in the reforestation programme.

The Consultancy department has carried out considerable research into waste management and large scale composting. This has provided essential information needed by Local Authorities in their work to reduce landfill.

Through the Information and Education department, the HDRA offers gardening advice not only to its ever-growing number of members but to the general public. It also runs courses on a wide range of related topics, as well as events for schools.

The HDRA is at the forefront in the campaign to reduce waste and improve the environment.

The Henry Doubleday Research Association
Ryton Organic Gardens,
Ryton-on-Dunsmore
Coventry
CV8 3LG
Tel. 01203 303517
Fax. 01203 639229

For further information about developing school grounds, contact Learning through Landscapes

Learning through Landscapes (LTL) promotes improvements to the environmental quality and educational use of school grounds by co-ordinating an imaginative programme of activities designed to encourage sustainable developments.

School grounds are vitally important outdoor spaces in an increasingly dangerous society. For most children they are the first public outdoor environment of which they have any sustained experience. Attitudes towards people and places are formed in them.

LTL is the only national organisation which deals with all aspects of school grounds development and, in this respect, is unique in the world.

We know, from our many research projects, that changes will only be sustainable if they are managed at local level. Our job, therefore, is to help individual schools to help themselves.

To do this, Learning through Landscapes:
- provides information and advice to headteachers, teachers, parents, governors, landscape architects, local authorities and anyone else who requests it
- produces publications to meet the needs of all those involved in school grounds development
- raises resources for innovative projects which help schools to implement changes
- carries out research to ensure that we are constantly able to give out the best advice
- runs a range of training courses, especially for headteachers, and works with other training organisations
- runs a number of membership schemes
- strives to ensure that the issue of school grounds is at the top of the agenda for educationalists and environmentalists.

This book is being promoted by LTL as part of the Green Releaf Primary Project, which is supported by the Department of the Environment under the Environmental Action Fund.

Learning through Landscapes Trust
Third Floor, Southside Offices
The Law Courts
Winchester
Hampshire
SO23 9DL
Tel. 01962 846258
Fax. 01962 869099

The Original
Wormery

The Purpose-built worm composter that aids the environment and produces liquid feed and rich organic compost.